SECRET MUSEUMS

GAUGUIN
&
M. VÁZQUEZ MONTALBÁN

Translated from Spanish
by Elisabeth Plaister

XIX
Century

FLOHIC
—EDITIONS—

UNENDING FLIGHT

Je vous accorde que l'artiste
n'aperçoit pas la Nature
comme elle apparaît au vulgaire,
puisque son émotion lui révèle
les vérités intérieures
sous les apparences.
Auguste Rodin - *L'Art*
(Entretiens réunis par Paul Gsell.)

I was of the opinion, in 1965, that flight was the perfect state for all beings, whether animal or human, and that we alone could ever hope to reach some place from which we would never wish to return. It became apparent that travel is to no avail for purposes of flight when we realize that on our travels we take ourselves along, in other words, we take along the very being we wish to get away from. The enormity of this thought has remained with me during my twenty-five years of writing. I began by planning a series of poems which inevitably brought me face to face with today's most symbolic fugitive, Paul Gauguin. Thus was born a

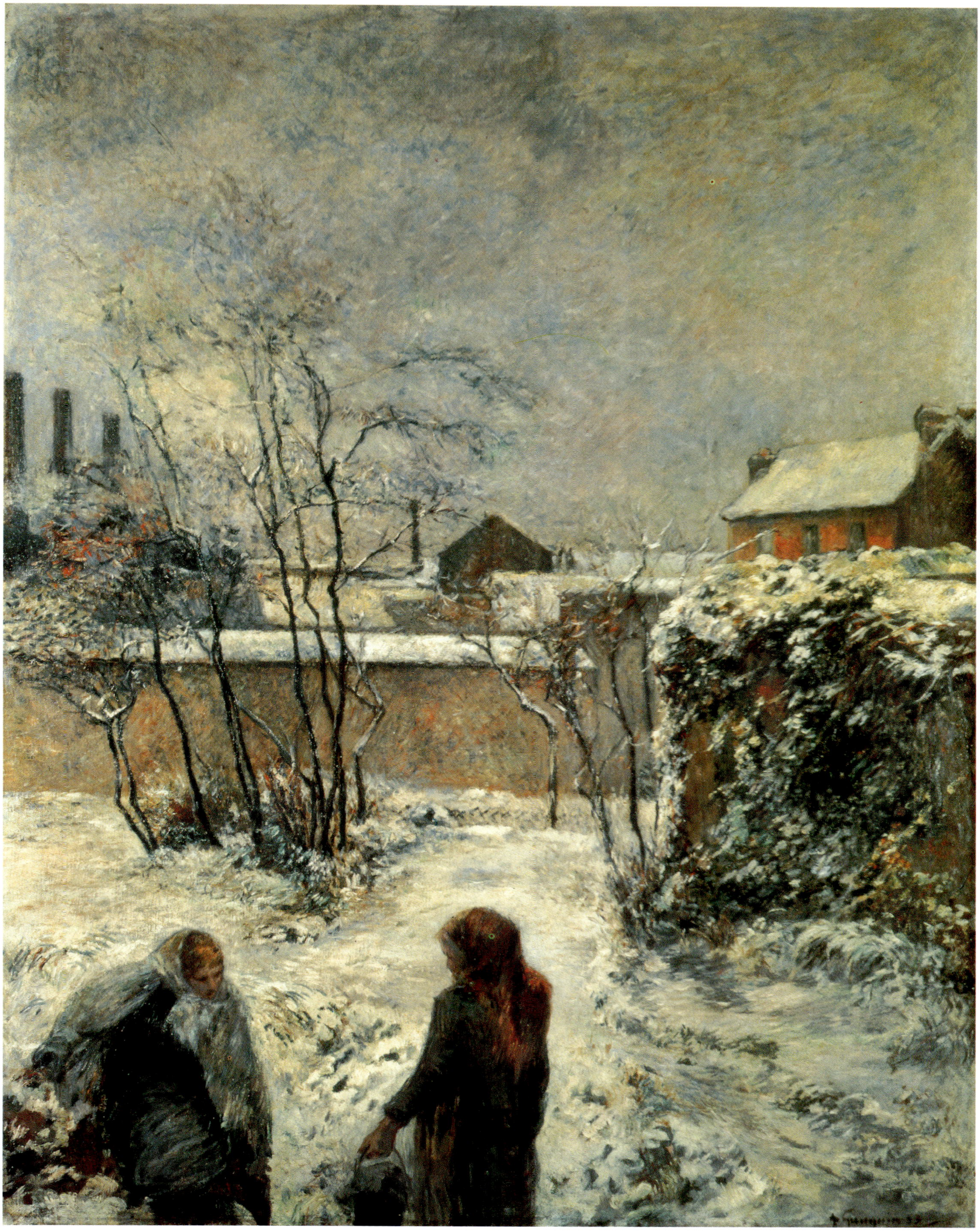

EFFET DE NEIGE - EFFECT OF SNOW
1883, Private collection
117 × 90 cm

poem published in the late 60's. The work was strongly influenced by the forms of narrative poetry and written in the style of Gottfried Benn's *Chopin*, the poem which served as my model for my travels in Gauguin's company:

Journalist
his father
wrote noteworthy articles
freedom — he said —
is a dignity of the people
but nonetheless
he died en route to Lima
where Paul was to turn six
one morning — at a quarter past eleven —
in June
eighteen hundred and fifty-four

My attempt to recapture Gauguin was neither onerous nor particularly far-sighted. The aim in the 60's was to achieve a democratic cultural and political order that was universal, decentralizing and anti-authoritarian. The left challenged the dialectic fatalism (or contradiction) which forces mankind to pass by way of slavery, feudalism and capitalism to reach socialism and repeated mention was made of the Asiatic mode of production giving rise to another potential emancipation process peculiar to a third world which has not undergone the industrial and liberal revolutions. We might

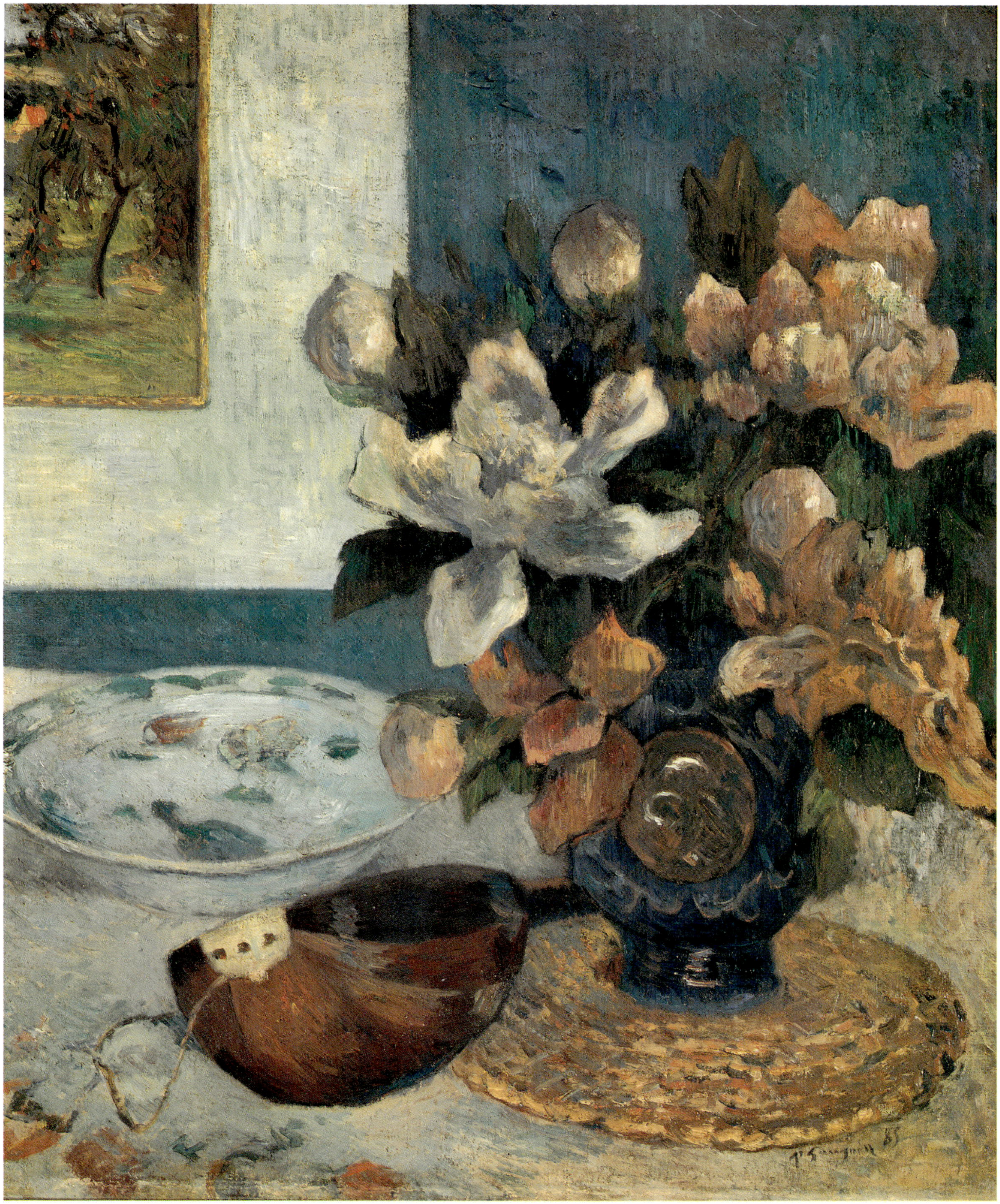

NATURE MORTE À LA MANDOLINE · STILL LIFE WITH MANDOLIN
1885, Paris, Musée d'Crsay
64 × 53 cm

recall how the word counterculture came into existence, as an alternative to the Western utilitarian awareness, and those droves fleeing from the system and seeking the other side of the moon in the South — which South is immaterial. They were called hippies and virtually all of them returned to the fold, as did those young revolutionaries who considered conventional Marxism to be inadequate and old hat and turned to Maoism as the radical extreme of contempt. During the 30's, the great Italian poet, Cesare Pavese, had written a disillusioned reflexion on the relative existence of the South as a promised alternative. This long poem bore the title "The South Seas" but nonetheless, thirty years later, new generations felt entitled to experience for themselves the illusion and disillusion of their own search for a personal South.

In time, this 60's preoccupation with the South served to boost tourism and underlay essential changes in the concept of dress, particularly female clothing. It also allowed UN and UNESCO linguists to turn the terms "North" and "South" into euphemisms for the dialectics of international exploitation, of slave and master. Gauguin at this stage was seen as a landmark pioneer of complex awareness, alternative in a contradictory manner, hardly linked in lore to fortune, protagonist merely in a black and white film version, played by George Sanders, of a Somerset Maugham's novel or in a necessarily technicolor film about his ambiguous and fauve relationship with Van Gogh in Arles.

I was attracted by Van Gogh's painting, by Gauguin's behaviour and, in writing my poems, I

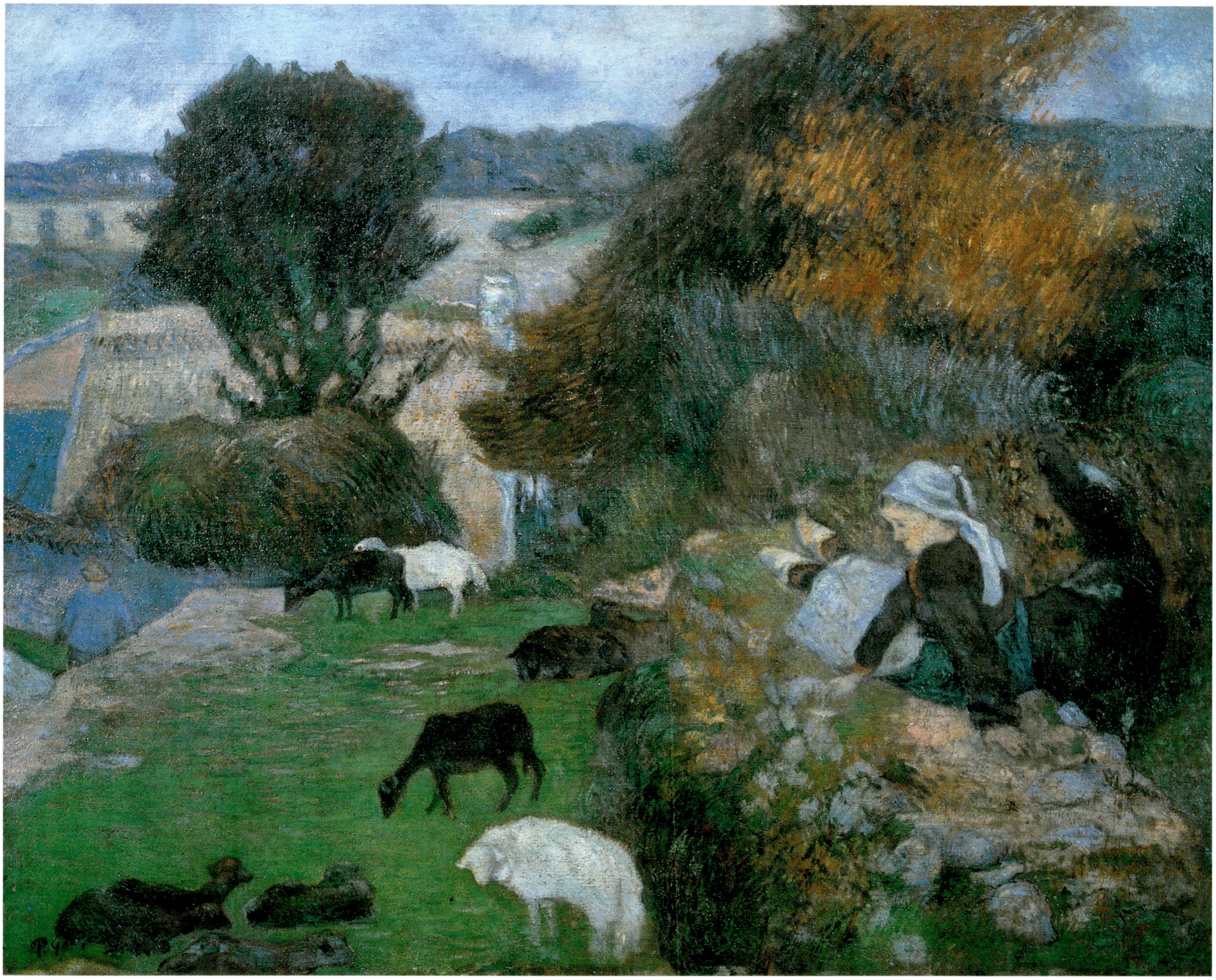

LA BERGÈRE BRETONNE · THE BRETON SHEPHERDESS
1886, Newcastle-upon-Tyne, Laing Art Gallery
60.4 × 73.3 cm

needed to go through writings on his opinions, as well as his most important letters, particularly those he wrote to Van Gogh and the latter's correspondence with his brother Theo. I witnessed a dual course between life and aesthetic intent that originally ran parallel and finally converged when the painter arrived in Tahiti in search of the "land of his childhood," to use Saint-Exupery's metaphor, and of the root of his artistic impulse. The "dark corners of the heart" in which Gauguin sometimes located the source of his artistic drive forced him to retrace the internal rationale of art and life to the point where he recovered his rocking horse, symbolic toy of a symbolic childhood: "I went back a long way, far beyond the Parthenon horses, to my childhood toy, my trusty rocking horse." In quest of his first glimpse of paradise lost, of nature as pretext for the expression of his perception, whether in the form of a woman, a tree, a dog or an object, Gauguin travelled the long road of painting as reflexion of reality and stopped short on the threshold of informalism, beyond which began irony or the downward slope towards dehumanization of art, for which spiritual incursions he felt no vocation.

Fifty-one years of life, a fairly normal biological journey — by 19th-century standards, — close to the average span calculated by health experts; a metaphorical journey, between two real journeys. The first, to Peru, began at two years of age in the company of his parents; the second, in 1895, to the Marquesas Islands, where he would die eight years later, with no immediate echo but the cry of Tioka, the old Kanaka native: "The white man is dead." His

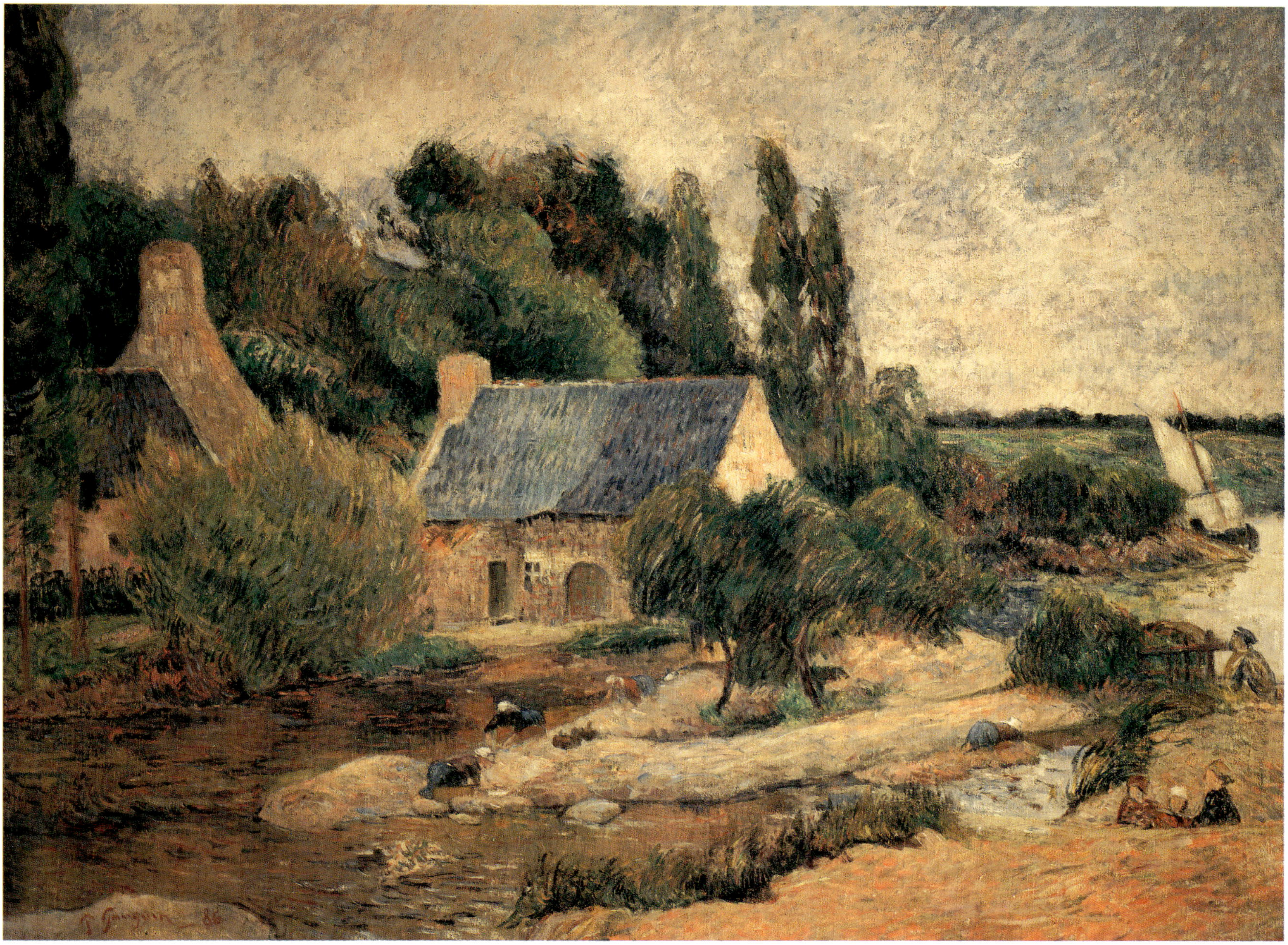

LES LAVANDIÈRES À PONT-AVEN - WASHERWOMEN IN PONT-AVEN
1886, Paris, Musée d'Orsay
71 × 90 cm

progressive journalist father, Clovis Gauguin, was disgusted by what he judged to be the inadequacy of the emancipating influence of the 1848 revolution and decided to seek a truly new world in Peru, home of his father-in-law. But this was not to be. Clovis Gauguin died on the journey and his wife, Aline Marie Chazal, sought the protection of her family upon their eventual arrival in Lima. This was no average family, although Paul may have been exaggerating when he claimed in *"Avant et Après"* that he was descended on his mother's side from a Borgia of Aragon, Viceroy of Peru. However, he was unquestionably the grandson of Flora Tristan, pioneer of utopian socialism and of feminism, personal friend of Fourier, Proudhon and George Sand who penned the fascinating memoirs *"Pilgrimages of an Outcast."* She died when Paul was four. He spent five golden years in Lima, in the bosom of the wealthy Moscoso family, spoilt and praised for his precocious talents, including an astonishing perceptive awareness of colour, smell and sound. The family's return to France, more specifically to Orléans, was a traumatic return to a mediocre life verging on poverty, in a dreary and cold landscape compared to that of Peru, beneath the dubious authority of a mother who never became an adult. She was to die young, in 1867, without having ever really understood her son. In her will she left her other children under the tutelage of Gustave Arosa but, with regard to Paul, she wrote: "My beloved son will have to forge his own future for he has never been able to win the affection of my friends and he will be left entirely

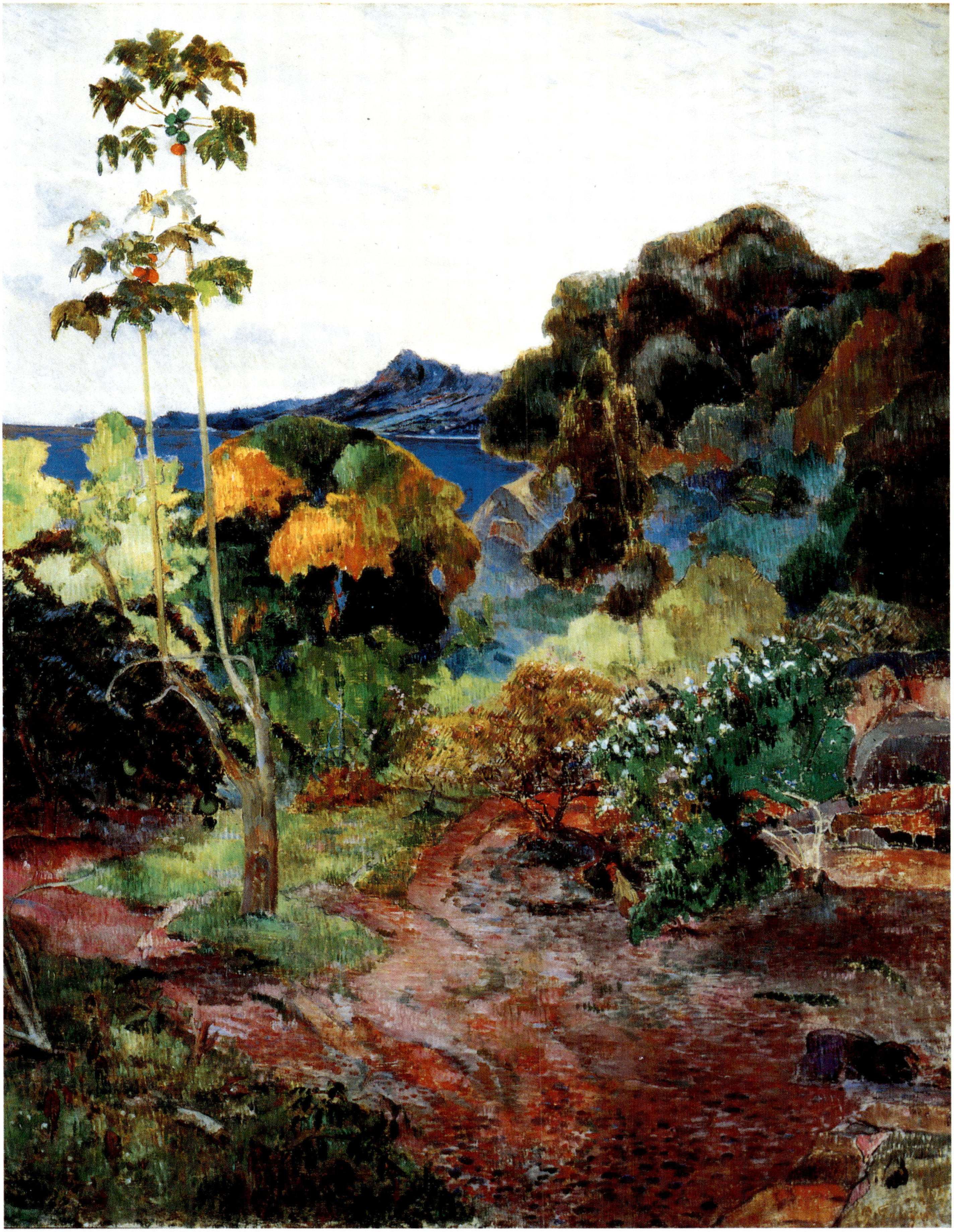

PAYSAGE DE LA MARTINIQUE - MARTINIQUE LANDSCAPE
(Tropical vegetation)
1887, Edinburgh, National Gallery of Scotland
116 × 89 cm

to his own resources." At the time, Paul was a nineteen-year-old pilot-in-training aboard a ship sailing the Atlantic. He would not return to France until 1871, after serving in the French navy during the Franco-Prussian War and taking a long-distance look at that first dress rehearsal for modern revolution, the Commune.

Returning ashore, he visited Gustave Arosa, an unusual individual acting both as a guardian to Paul's brothers and sisters and as a businessman, a great collector of leading impressionist painters, particularly of Pissarro who was the most politically-committed of those young "rejected" painters. It was in the home of this cultured bourgeois that Gauguin discovered the new painting, *the only painting,* producing an emotional turmoil that changed the course of his life. It was also Arosa who set him up in a very lucrative job in a stockbroker's office, introduced him to Pissarro and critiqued Gauguin's first canvases when he was still a naive, amateur painter who began his apprenticeship by imitating the Impressionists. Pissarro considered Impressionism to be the aesthetics of progressivism, based on a notion of progress that is both accumulative and self-surpassing, figuring in the dialectic rationale of continuous material and spiritual growth. Any vanguard resolves, in synthesis, the conflict between tradition and revolution and implies a certain conception of life, history and art.

There is no need to dwell on biographical information covering the conventional story of his life: that he married a young Danish woman, Mette;

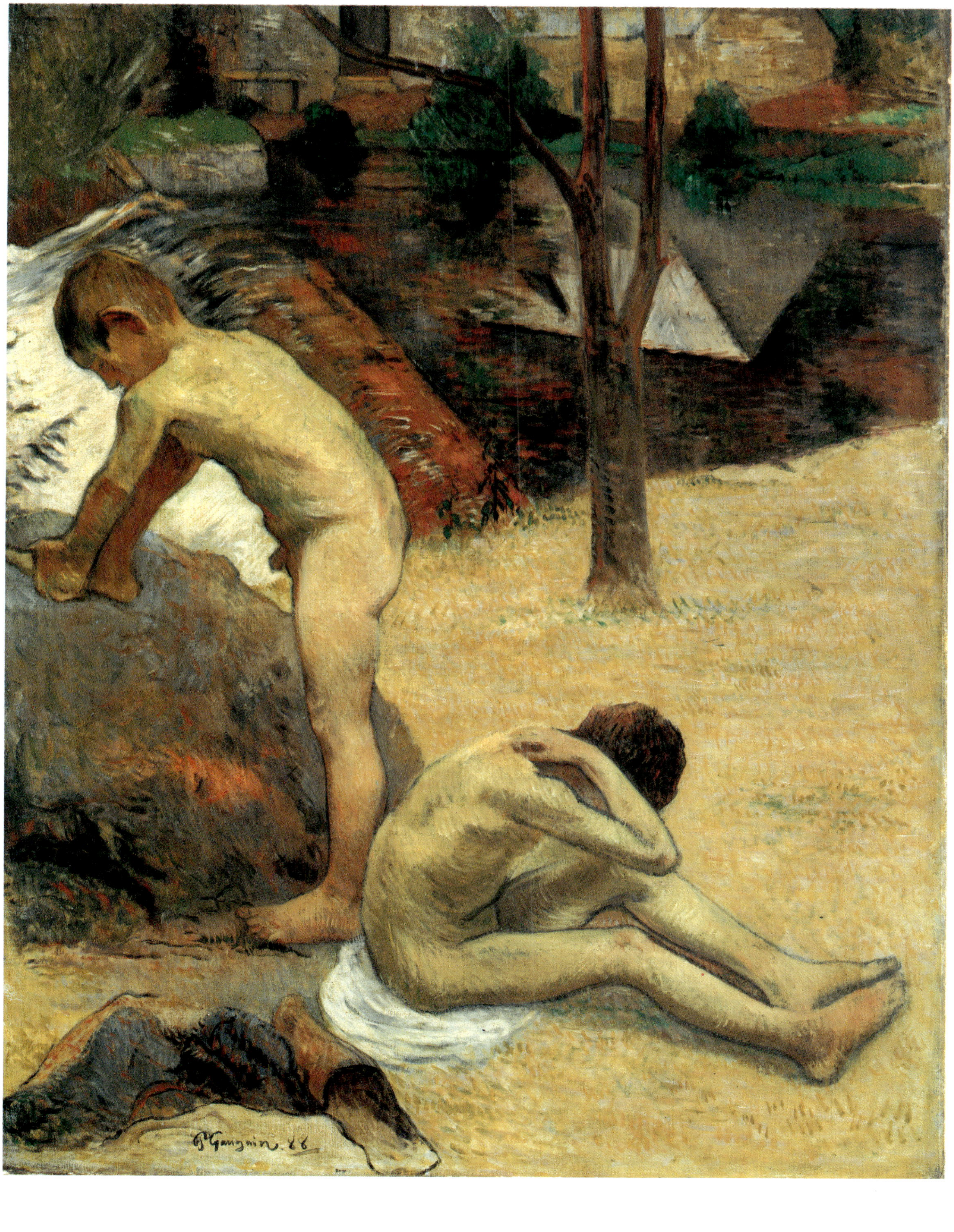

JEUNES BAIGNEURS BRETONS - YOUNG BRETON BATHERS
1888, Hamburg, Hamburgerkunsthalle
92 × 73cm

that they had five children; that he lived a comfortable bourgeois life until he decided in 1883 to devote himself solely to painting, after receiving encouraging comments on the paintings he exhibited in the Impressionist galleries. Gauguin embraced his situation as "refused" artist because his stockbroker persona was but a varnish over the being whose thirst for travel was never quenched, and who was ready to sacrifice bourgeois comfort, family or anything else that held him back as he ventured forth to discover his painting and himself. From his stable bourgeois past he retained a tendency to become depressed whenever he found himself out of funds (more often than not), whence his harping on financial problems despite the fact that he had chosen a way of life that virtually guaranteed penury. It is not true that he was indifferent to his separation from Mette and his children. He followed their doings, from a distance, anxious to know how they were faring since he could contribute nothing to their welfare, ignoring his rejection by Mette's family who saw Gauguin as a harebrained and immoderate Southerner. The premature deaths of his children, Aline and Clovis, sank him further into physical and moral decay during the last years of his life in Polynesia and he never ceased deceiving himself that he might one day be able to return to a stable life with his family.

Gauguin was rebellious, quarrelsome, conceited, manipulative. His art matured in proximity to Pissarro and Degas, his mind was exercised by the literature produced by the perverse post-Baudelairean culture, in personal contact with the poets and

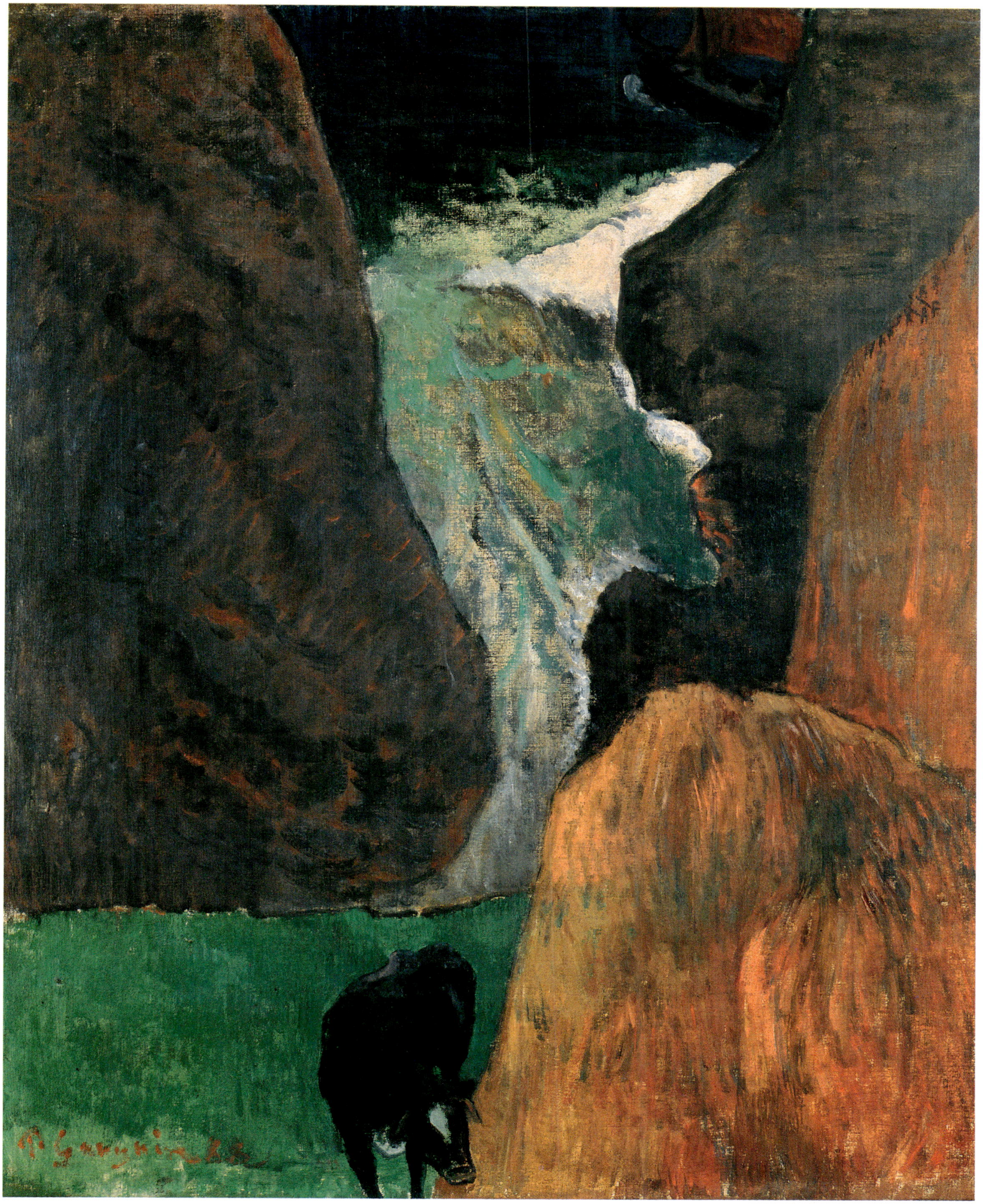

MARINE AVEC VACHES AU-DESSUS DU GOUFFRE - MARINA WITH COWS OVER THE ABYSS
1888, Paris, Musée des Arts décoratifs
73 × 60 cm

critics of the vanguard who might readily be encountered in the Parisian cafés known for their stimulating gatherings, such as the Brasserie Andler, the Voltaire, the Tarenne, the Nouvelle-Athènes. He was particularly drawn to the gatherings in the Voltaire where first Mirbeau and later Mallarmé expressed their admiration for his genius which was a prerequisite for winning his friendship. Gauguin is one of the few artists able to theorize on his own paintings and he was a tireless writer of letters and articles which were generally in the nature of self-clarification, to which end he used the support of painters who had contact with him or followed in his footsteps: Laval, Bernard, even Van Gogh. He went so far as to produce lengthy writings, particularly during the last years of his life, when he felt that his conception of the world and his art, his means of dominating that world, were firmly established. Certain of his manuscripts, such as *Ancien Culte mahorie, Avant et Après, L'Esprit moderne du catholicisme* and *Noa Noa,* together with his voluminous correspondence, shed light on Gauguin's philosophy in which life and painting converge upon the long road to self-knowledge.

Individualistic, increasingly anti-social and irresponsible, Gauguin would readily be classified by a sociologist as a conservative anarchist, which was indeed Françoise Cachin's social diagnosis of the painter. Hauser, on the other hand, assigned him to decadent bohemia, spawned by Baudelaire, bohemians and fugitives through travel for its own sake, anti-establishment. "Both arise out of individualism and romantic irreality." But a distinction should be

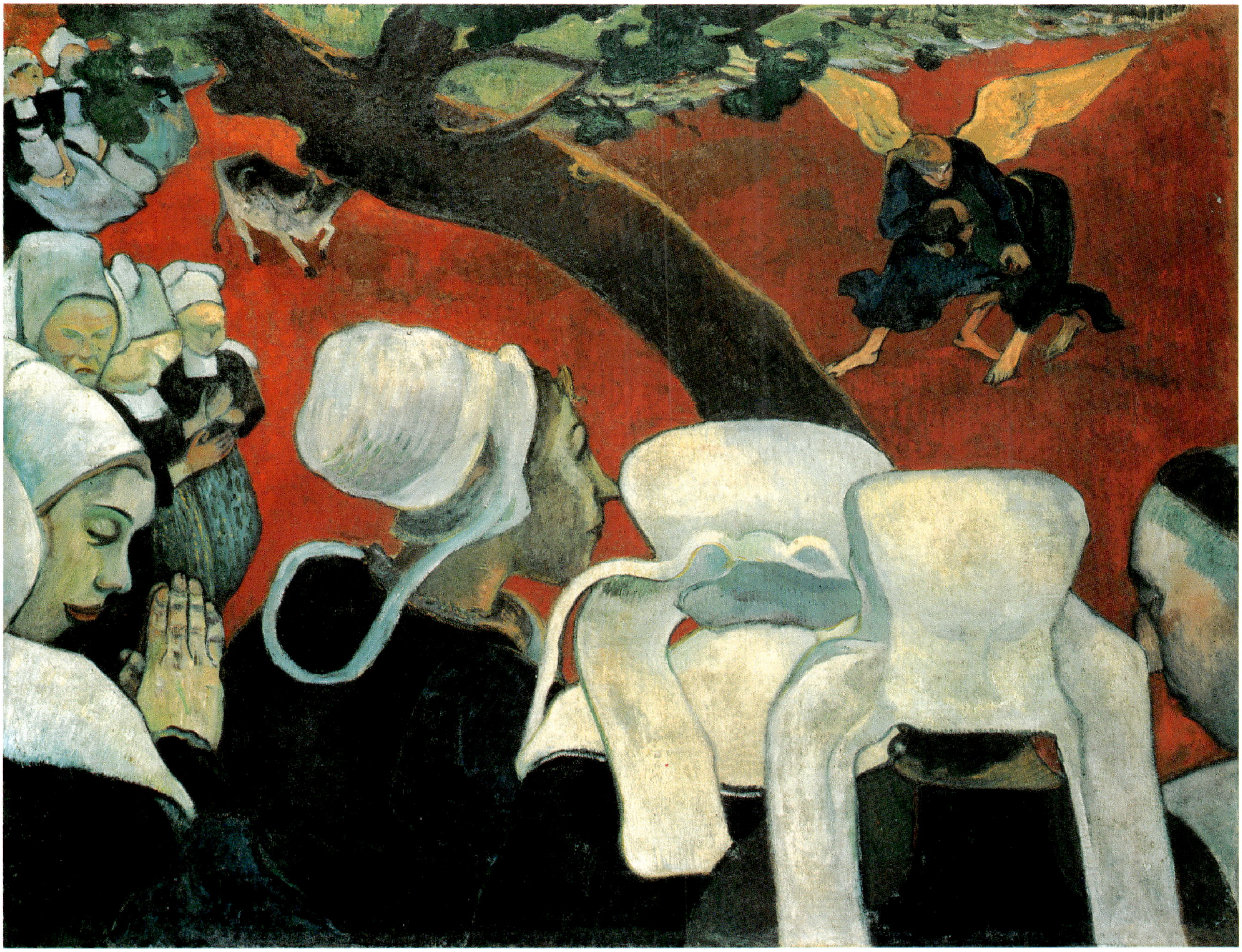

LA VISION APRÈS LE SERMON - VISION AFTER THE SERMON
(or Jacob's struggle with the Angel)
1888, Edinburgh, National Gallery of Scotland
73 × 92 cm

made between the bohemian and the snob fugitive of Baudelaire's ilk:

But the only real travellers are those who
depart for the sake of departing,

acting out the hypothesis of rebellion against conformist society, acting out the role of bohemian and fugitive for whom marginalization and travel are the only recourse, which was frequently the position of poor artists during the last quarter of the 19th century. Gauguin had no need to conjure up the antagonistic bourgeois conformism, he found it in his home when he attempted to return to family life. Mette's relatives were horrified by this artist who refused to bow to the laws of the market, who barely earned a living and caused his wife and children to live in poverty. He never travelled for the sake of it, he travelled as much under the dictates of financial or artistic necessity, whether it be the orphaned state that took him to Peru, or his poverty in Paris which triggered his trips to Brittany or Arles, as much as to seek a naturalist primitivism not to be found in Paris. He betrayed no hint of addiction to "le malheur du siècle," that abstract anguish engendered by a repugnance for bourgeois society and a quest for truth allied with a fear of the truth: "Who knows but that the truth may be sad," wrote Renan, and Rimbaud made it all the more difficult still: "What is not known may well be terrible." Gauguin experienced the very real anguish of hunger and not being able to pay the rent, but he held on to the positive purpose of his uprooting and departure: he was seeking his artistic truth while he forged an undefined idealization of

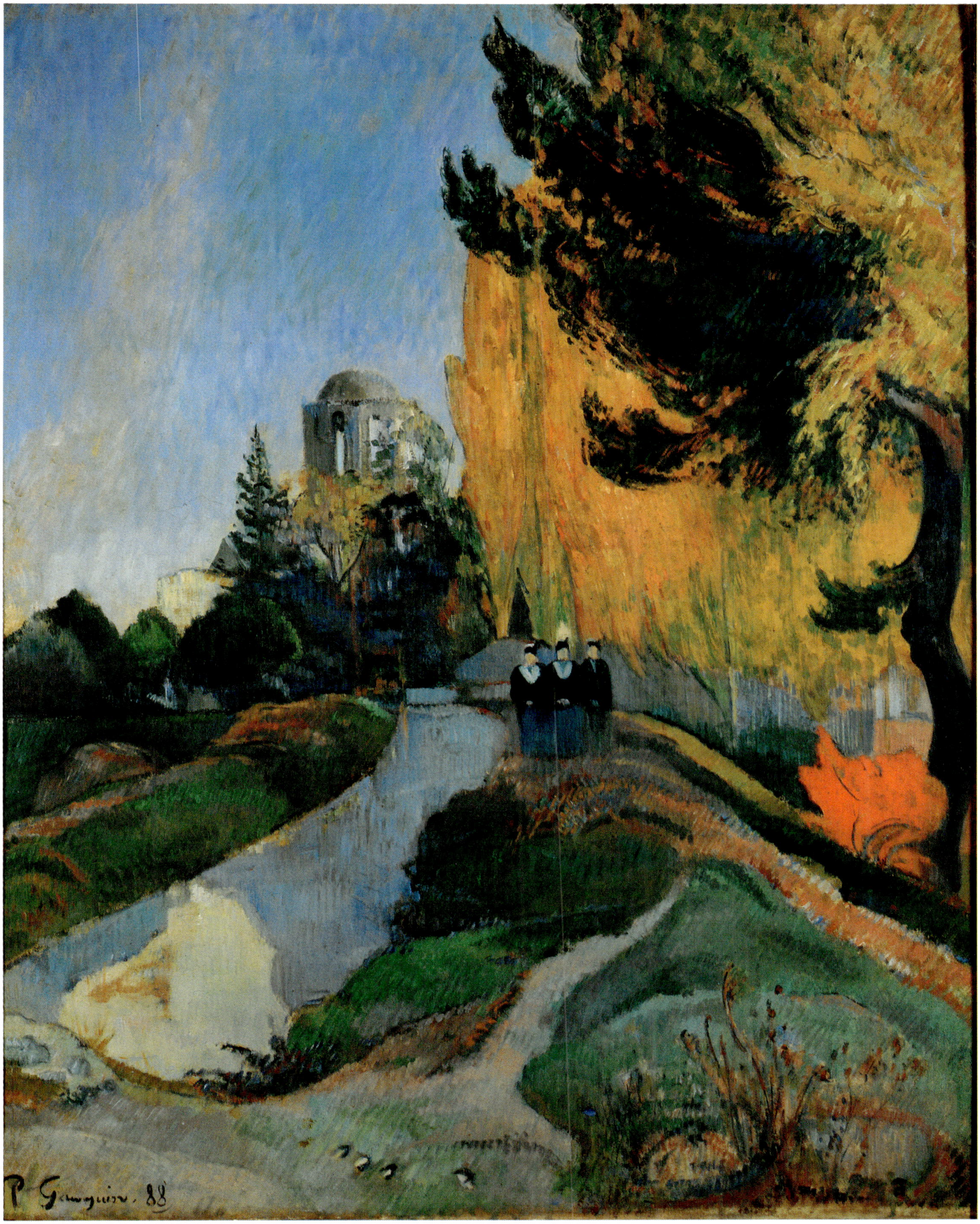

THE ALYSCAMPS
1888, Paris, Musée d'Orsay
92 × 73cm

himself. His appropriation of the would-be paradise of the noble savage is not so much a rationalized rejection of bourgeois and imperialist Europe as a desire to identify an innocent pictorial outlook with an innocent nature. He occasionally put forward an ideological interpretation of his social position, inevitably ceding under the weight of conventional conformist truths, as when he dedicated what can only be called a political diatribe in written form to his wife: "There are two classes in society, one which possesses wealth from birth, allowing the individual to become a financier, employee under contract or businessman, and another which possesses no wealth. What should the latter live on? On the fruits of their labour." Gauguin adds that the artist is the finest element of the nation, bearing its fruits, enriching it: "You do not love art. So what do you love? Money." Hangover of an ex-stockbroker fallen into bad ways or result of a rare objectivizing moment of the class struggle, his own aesthetic quest countered any suspicion of active political involvement. This would have required him to give a place in his life to others and to otherness, holding him back against his will in his unceasing travels and distracting him from his creative self-absorption. When he was painting *La Danse des quatre Bretonnes* in Pont-Aven, he claimed to be transcending the naturalist reality of his models, involving a concentrated study of the relationship between form and colour as media in themselves. Pissarro's reaction was critical, reproving him for assimilating formalizations of Japanese and Byzantine art without integrating their syntheses "with our

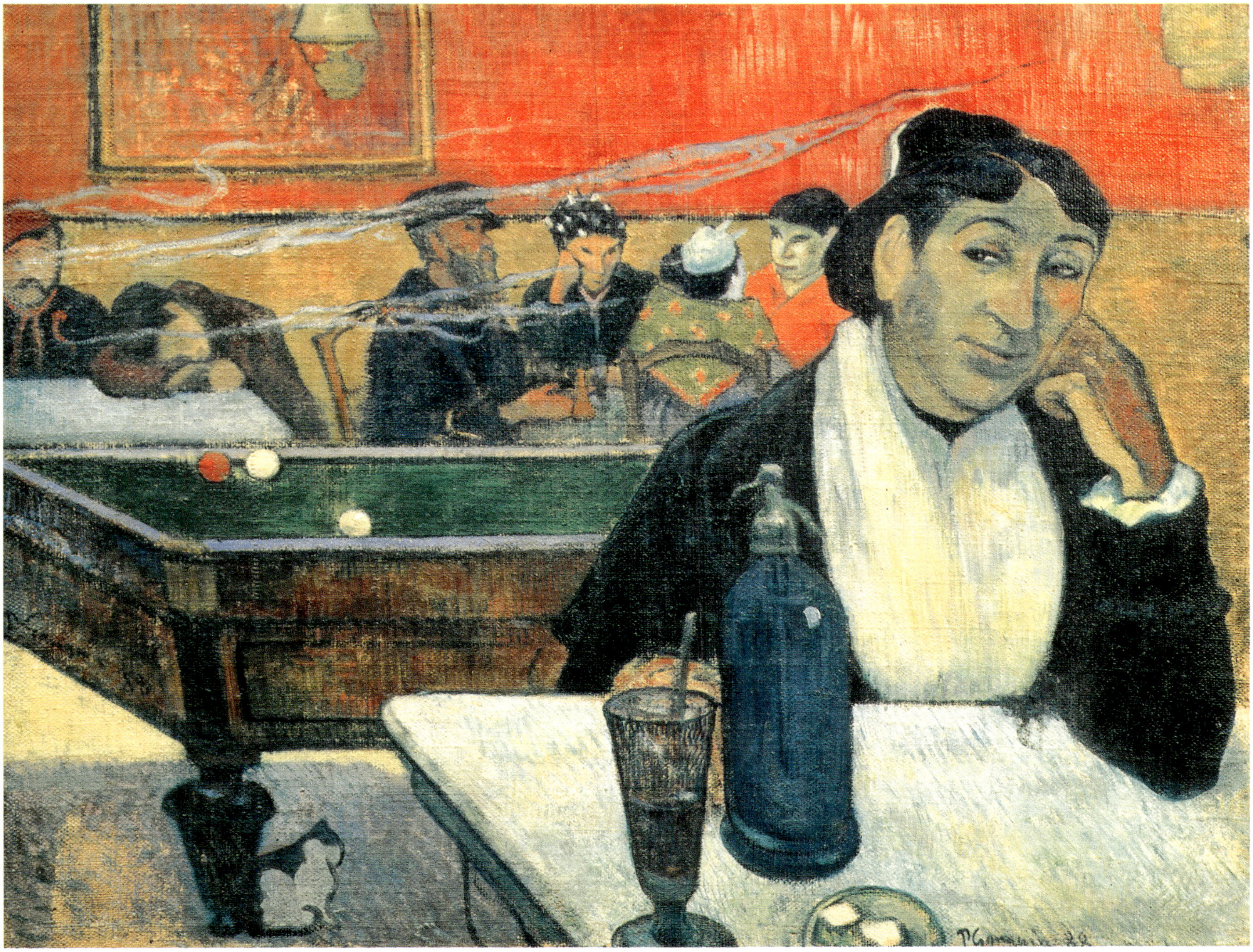

IN THE CAFÉ
(Mrs Ginoux)
1888, Moscow, Pushkin Museum
73 × 92 cm

modern philosophy which is completely social, anti-authoritarian and antimystical. That is the worst of it. It is a step backwards, Gauguin is not a clairvoyant, he is a slick operator who has perceived that the bourgeoisie is ceding, retreating before the great solidary ideas that are germinating in the heart of the people — an unconscious idea but the only legitimate one! The Symbolists are in the same situation."

It was not necessary for Pissarro to cast Gauguin out from a progressive interpretation of art going hand in hand with a choice of explicitly communicable subjects. He had never felt himself to be the revealer of a real or social situation, rather a user of bodies and objects with a view to attaining an artistic truth which was self-absorbed, although with a conscious symbolistic decantation, he would eventually come to lay down a full programme of metaphysical enigmas: *Where do we come from? What are we? Where are we going?* But if we were to deprive this latter emblematic picture of the meaning revealed by its title, we would take away none of its fundamental value and it would be interpreted as a Polynesian representation of the earthly paradise or as a South Seas' *Déjeuner sur l'herbe*. The discomfort engendered by an irreversible utilitarian society was no longer naively romantic but had become antagonistic: the negating awareness of conventional Good and the celebration of Evil as offence to the established utilitarian morality, make Baudelaire the creator of modern perversity. In a brief but very intense study on Baudelaire, included in *Literature and Evil*, Bataille

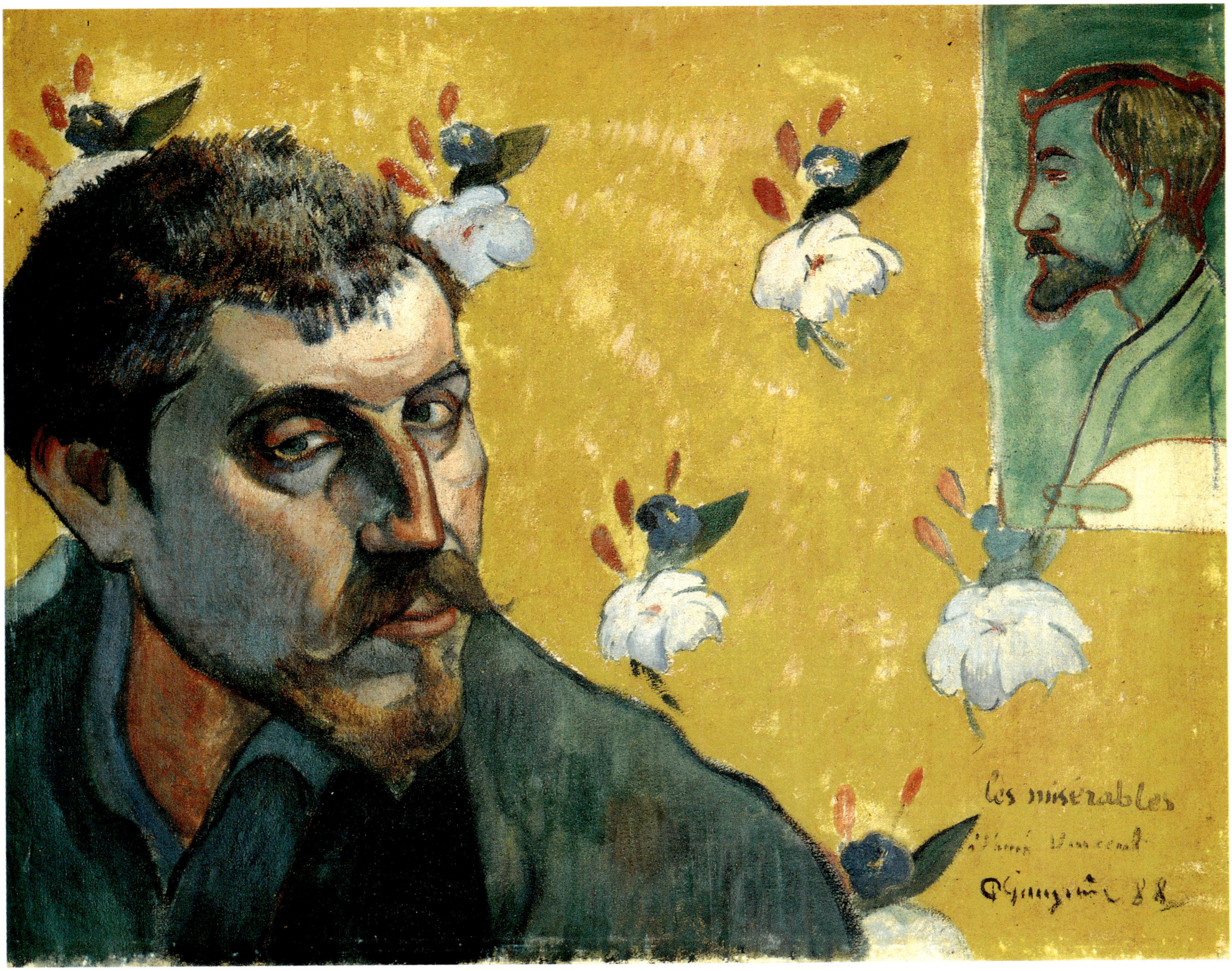

LES MISÉRABLES
1888, Amsterdam, Rijksmuseum Vincent Van Gogh
45 × 55 cm

draws a distinction between Baudelaire's nihilistic rebellion and the social protest channelled through the workers' movement. Baudelaire's post-Romantic perversity rejects utilitarianism but fails to propose an alternative historical meaning and, instead, capitalists and members of the proletariat will have to believe in control of this utilitarianism if they are to possess the future. Gauguin's position, however, contains but a hint of this Baudelairean complicity and constitutes a third alternative whereby the artist shakes off nihilistic despair and utilitarian hope through self-absorption and nostalgia for natural pre-utilitarian conduct. Gauguin sought to compensate for all this in his flights to Panama, Martinique, Brittany and the South Seas, hence reflecting a degree of confidence in the existence of residual paradises to act as models for his art and make nonsense of the choice between despairing nihilism and the return of the triumphant conformist morality.

This singular moral position assumed by Gauguin and others who opted for flight adds to the difficulty of classifying them by clearly-defined schools. When he ceased to be explicitly impressionist, Gauguin entered an undefined poetic realm which every art historian or theorist has sought to fit into contemporary or subsequent categories. Symbolist. Fauve. Accessory to the ornamentality of Art Nouveau. Pre-Cubist. Gauguin had been gradually, spontaneously, moving away from Impressionism, but effected a definite break when Seurat made a bid to turn it into a science of the picture. He was certainly developing towards a flat artistic represen-

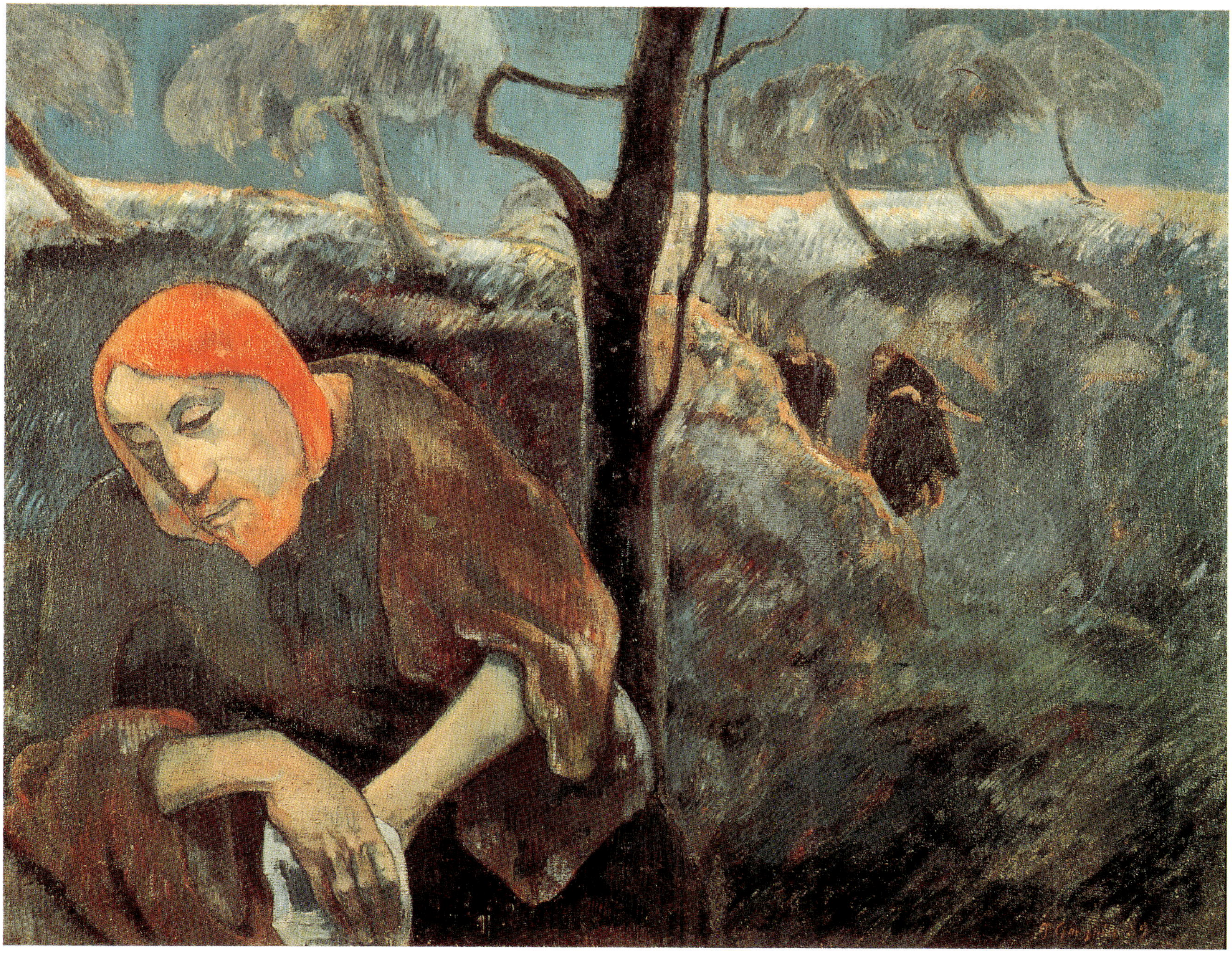

LE CHRIST AU JARDIN DES OLIVIERS · CHRIST IN THE OLIVE GROVE
1889, West Palm Beach, Norton Gallery
73 × 92 cm

tation, with his shapes contoured in pre-geometric outlines. From Cézanne he took no more than a couple of apples from certain pictures and admired his development while not identifying with a style which denies subjectivity and seeks the autonomous objectivity of the pictorial syntax, which denies nature in the process of reducing it to its geometric soul. Seurat and Cézanne, along with their friend and critic Pissarro, are effectively utilitarian, opting to believe in the application of continuous growth of the spirit in the cultural preserve of painting and committing themselves to the rationale of vanguards capable of outdistancing past periods of seeing and depicting. Seurat handed the torch to Cézanne, who passed it on to Braque, Picasso, Gris, finally to undergo the essential revolution effected by Kandinsky. Gauguin, however, stood on the sidelines of this object-based rationale, developing towards a naif morality through a naif aesthetic code which is not readily transferable, less so than even Van Gogh's schizophrenic art. It was a point of reference to which the Expressionists laid claim, although Fauves and Modernists were also influenced by its colour and decorative nature, as were the Nabists in its guise as a post-Symbolist landmark.

Gauguin not only defended the interpretation of nature as model but also the fact that painting should be allowed to transmit an idea symbolically. Although theorizing is not his strong point, he does shed sufficient light on the theory underlying his work. Many of the de-ideologizing painters who admired his work played down his efforts at sym-

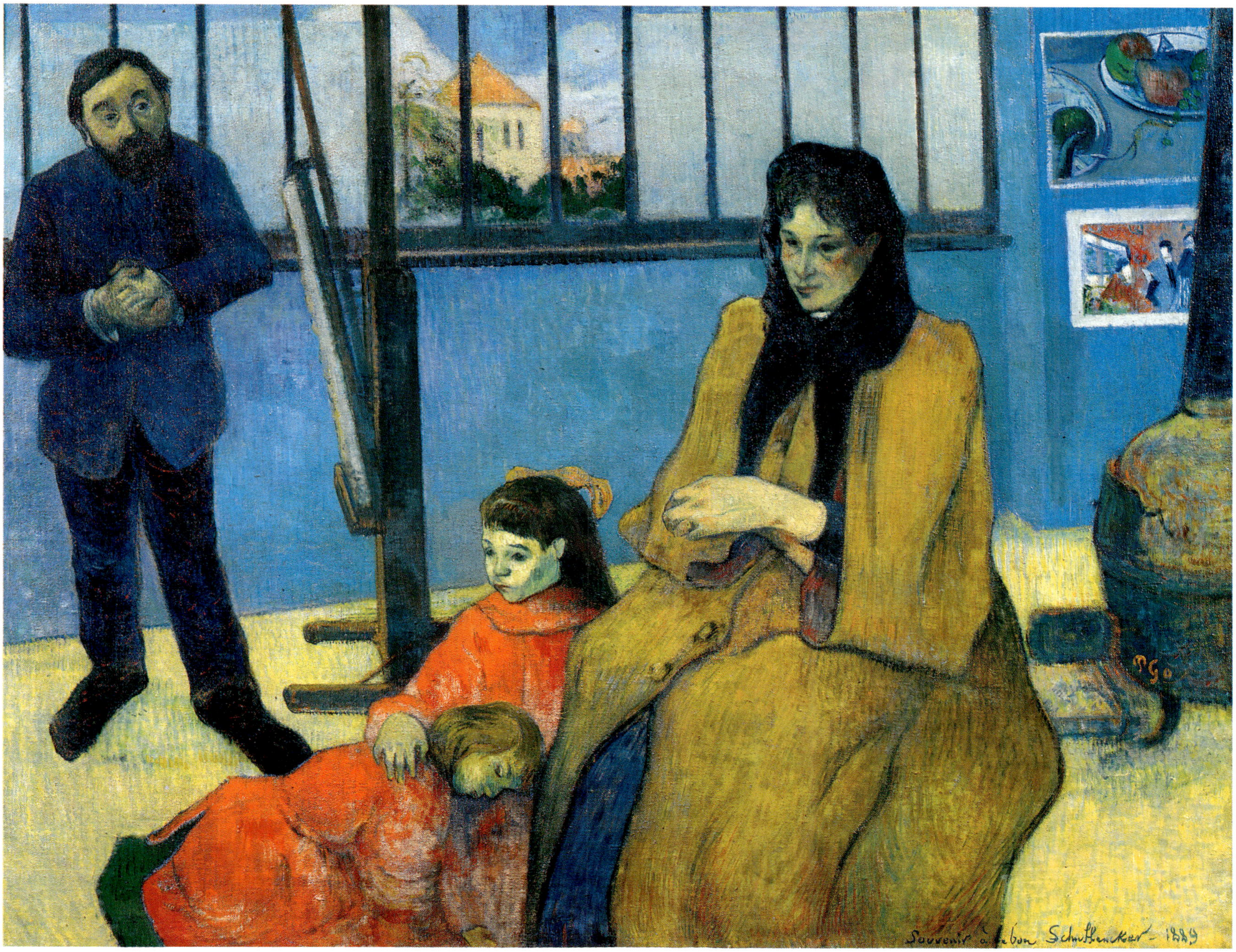

LA FAMILLE SCHUFFENECKER - THE SCHUFFENECKER FAMILY
1889, Paris, Musée d'Orsay
73 × 92 cm

bolism and meaning; Matisse in *Ecrits et Propos sur l'Art* lauded him, alongside Cézanne, primarily for his innovative use of colour: "From Delacroix to Van Gogh and particularly Gauguin, by way of the Impressionists who made a good job of cleaning up, and of Cézanne who took the final plunge and introduced volumes of colour, it is possible to follow step by step the reinstatement of the function of colour, the restitution of its emotive force." Emotive and symbolic, Gauguin would no doubt add, under the influence of Mallarmé's discourses on the symbolic colour of words, although he was never overly impressed by Mallarmé's poems. Alistair Mackintosh, in *Symbolism and Art Nouveau*, attempts to attribute to Gauguin his deserved symbolism, duly differentiated from Pre-Raphaelite symbolism and Munch's expressionism. Mackintosh considers that Gauguin did not realize his full creative potential until he encountered a type of nature reflecting exciting cultures, suggesting colours that symbolize such a peculiarity. Hence his reason for seeking realities that had not been vulgarized by the bourgeois quest for development which was more firmly entrenched in "backward" and reactionary Brittany than in Paris which was posing for the painters of the world. Gauguin's attitude in seeking primitivism should not be confused with that of the Pre-Raphaelites who sought their inspiration and style in a culturalized primitivism, nurtured by the cultured emotions awoken in them by the painters preceding Raphael, in conjunction with excessively literary or over-idealized arguments.

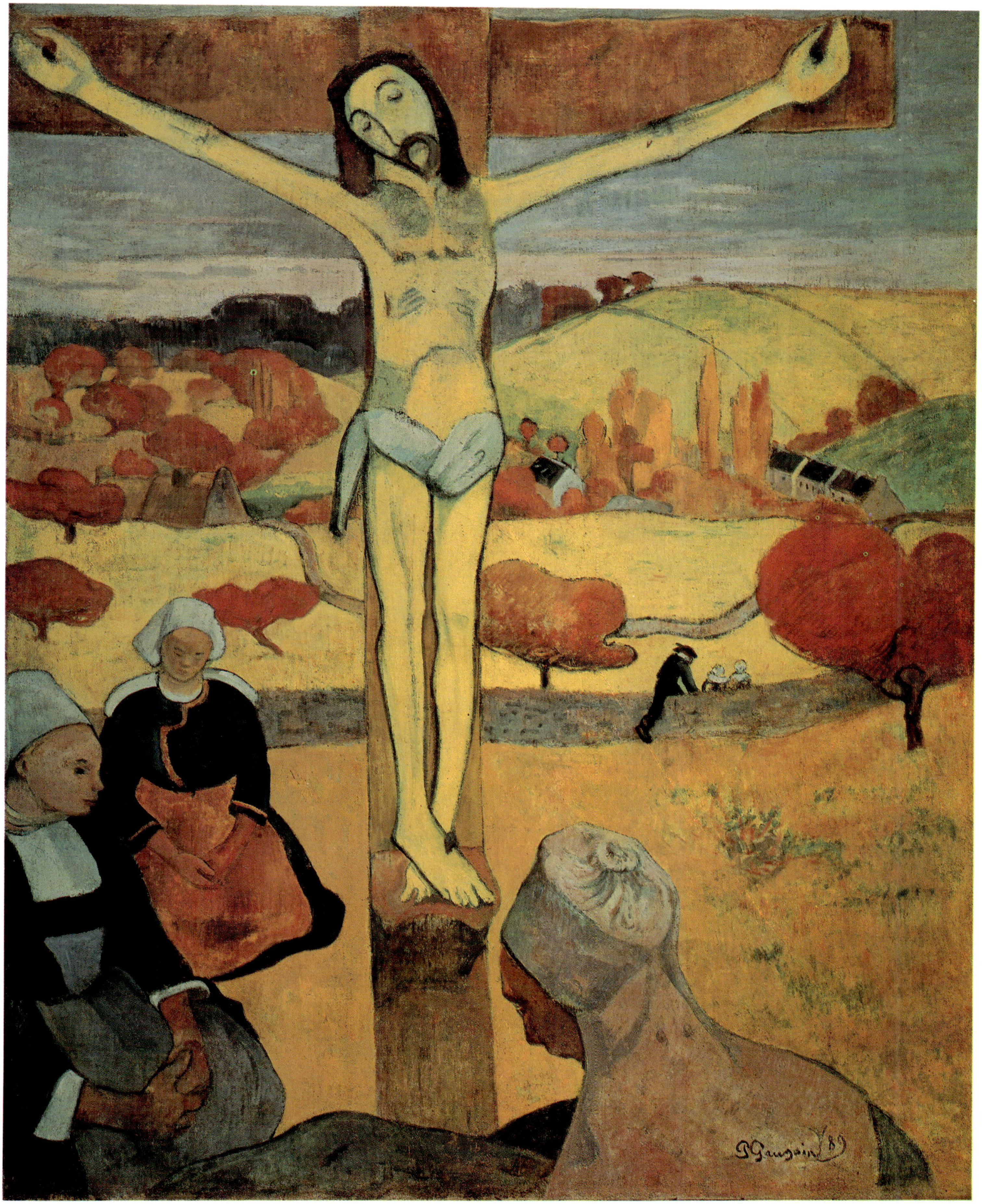

LE CHRIST JAUNE - THE YELLOW CHRIST
1889, Buffalo, Albright-Knox Art Gallery
92 × 73 cm

When required to explain to Schuffenecker what he was endeavouring to communicate in one of his quintessential paintings, *Les Misérables*, which appears to be a self-portrait dedicated to Van Gogh, he gives abundant clues to the nature of his current poetic view, although he still calls himself an "impressionist": "I think this is one of my most successful efforts; it is abstract to the point of being incomprehensible... First the head of a very dubious character, a Jean Valjean [the protagonist of *Les Misérables*] personifying an impressionist painter of ill repute [Gauguin himself] who is simultaneously weighed down by the chains of the world. The drawing is totally individual; it is a complete abstraction. The eyes, mouth and nose are like flowers on a Persian rug, conveying the symbolic aspect. The colour is totally unrealistic, imagine a chaotic collection of china all twisted by the heat of the oven! All the reds and purples striped by tongues of flame like a fully-stoked oven, radiating from the eyes, abode of the painter's mental strife. The whole against a chrome yellow background sprinkled with childish posies. The dwelling place of a pure maiden. Such is Impressionism, as yet unsullied by the fetid kiss of the Académie des Beaux-Arts." The modern reader is surprised by Gauguin's ready use of the terms abstract, symbolist and impressionist. Effectively, the three definitions as applied to art today no longer mean exactly what they did in Gauguin's time. "Impressionism" today is associated basically with a moment in the artistic renovation of ideological and technical reality. It was during this same period, in 1868, that

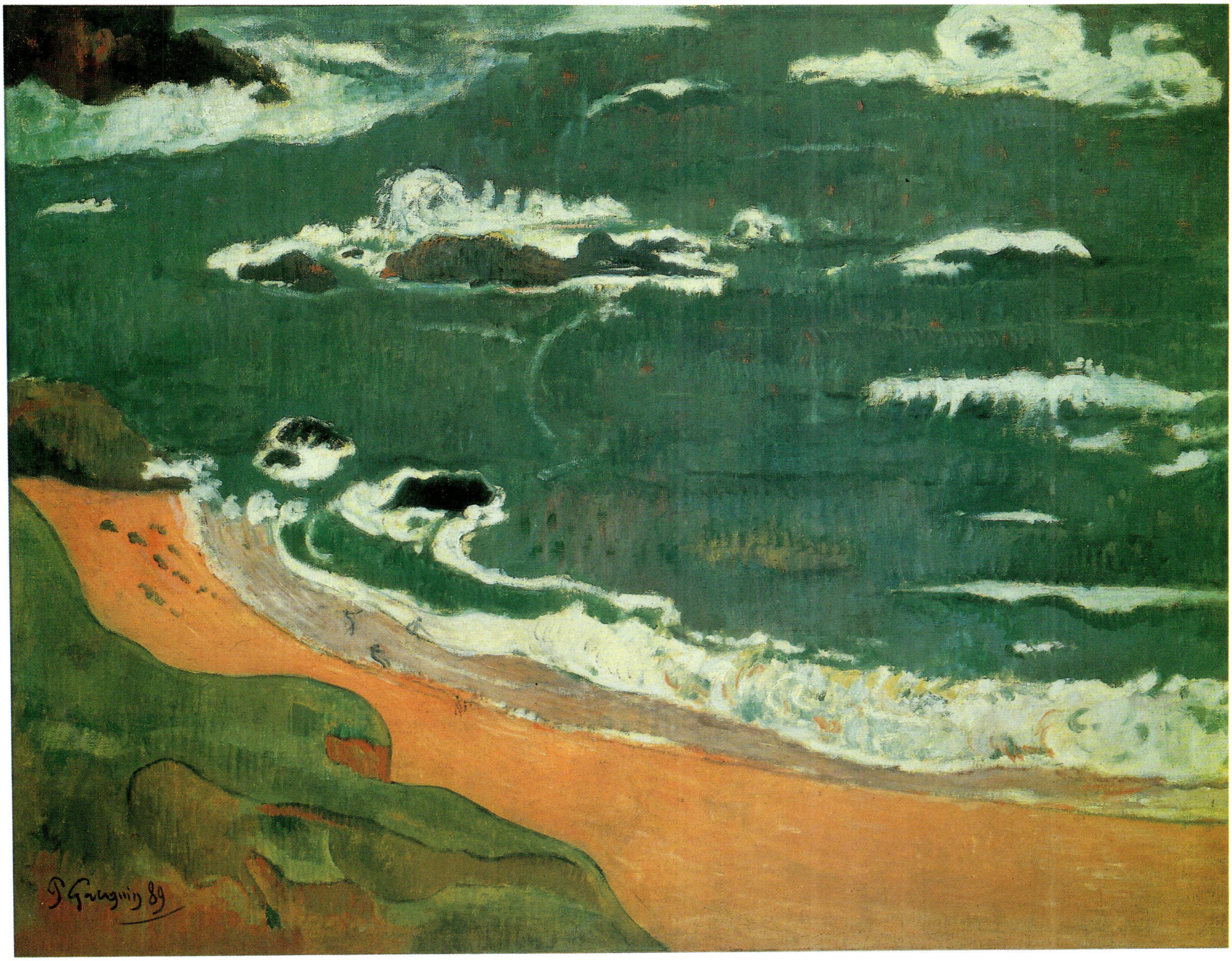

LA PLAGE DU POULDU - POULDU BEACH
1889, Private collection
73 × 92 cm

Zola called Monet and Renoir "actualists": "Painters who love their own period from the bottom of their artistic minds and souls," as opposed to the culturism and historicism of reactionary academic painting. They came onto the scene offering a blend of social and visual realism through an atomic decomposition of the pictorial mass, opening the way ultimately to Seurat. A painting did not, however, have to be an exact reproduction, photography existed for this purpose, and could therefore permit the play of the painter's own filtered view aiming to impress the receiver: "In his works, the Impression is what counts," states the critic Castagnary on the subject of the Dutch painter Jongkind's exhibition in 1863. Théophile Gautier regretted that a certain painter was content to create an impression "and neglected detail." Two years later, in 1865, Daubigny called this same painter "leader of the school of impression," although the most notable Impressionist painters preferred to be called "the rejected" because their works were exhibited in the "Salon des Refusés." It is to this Impressionism that Gauguin refers when he gives himself this artistic label at a time when, according to the recriminatory Pissarro, he had already foresaken orthodox Impressionism, in the sense that he sought to drum up the subjective complicity of the impressed receiver and, said Pissarro, his treatment of idea, form and colour were much more subversive than that of the regular Impressionists, to the extent that it became a new academic trend or the basis of a new science of painting, in other words, of perception, through Seurat's pointillism. This was after the critics had

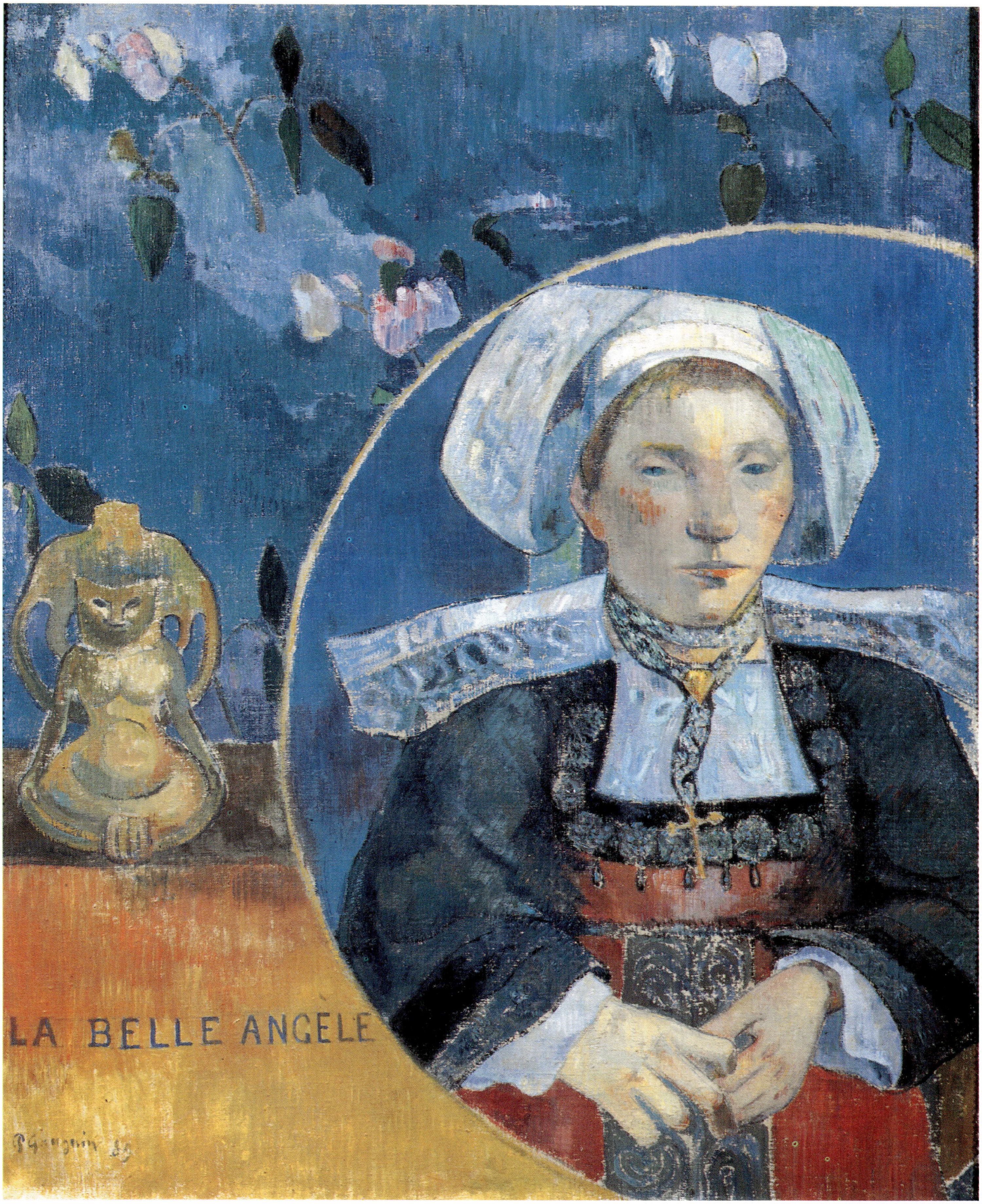

LA BELLE ANGÈLE - THE BEAUTIFUL ANGELA
1889, Paris, Musée d'Orsay
92 × 73 cm

coined the pejorative term "impressionists" for those who had declared war on beauty.

Gauguin's symbolism appeared to be awaiting Carl G. Jung's conceptual clarification in *Man and His Symbols*: "What we call symbol is a term, a name, even a painting that can be familiar in everyday life, even though it has specific connotations over and above its normal and obvious meaning." He goes on to write in almost exact keeping with Gauguin's poetic line: "As scientific knowledge has accumulated, so has our world become increasingly dehumanized. Man feels isolated in the cosmos, because he no longer feels a part of nature and has lost his emotive "unconscious identity" with natural phenomena. These have gradually lost their symbolic connotations. Thunder is no longer the voice of an angry god, nor lightning his instrument of retribution. Rivers contain no spirits and neither is the tree the vital origin of man, there is no snake that is wisdom incarnate, and no devil inhabits the cave on the mountainside. No voices are to be heard issuing from stones, from plants, from animals, nor does man speak to them in the belief that they can hear him. Man's contact with nature has been lost and, with it, the emotive strength afforded by these symbolic relations."

Gauguin, however, attempted to counteract this loss, seeking instinctively symbolic realities. As Pissarro maintained, this was actually a step backwards, but it allowed him to execute his best work. It was the reverse journey to that travelled by the oneiric symbolism of artificial and dehumanized surrealism, be it secular in nature or grotesquely

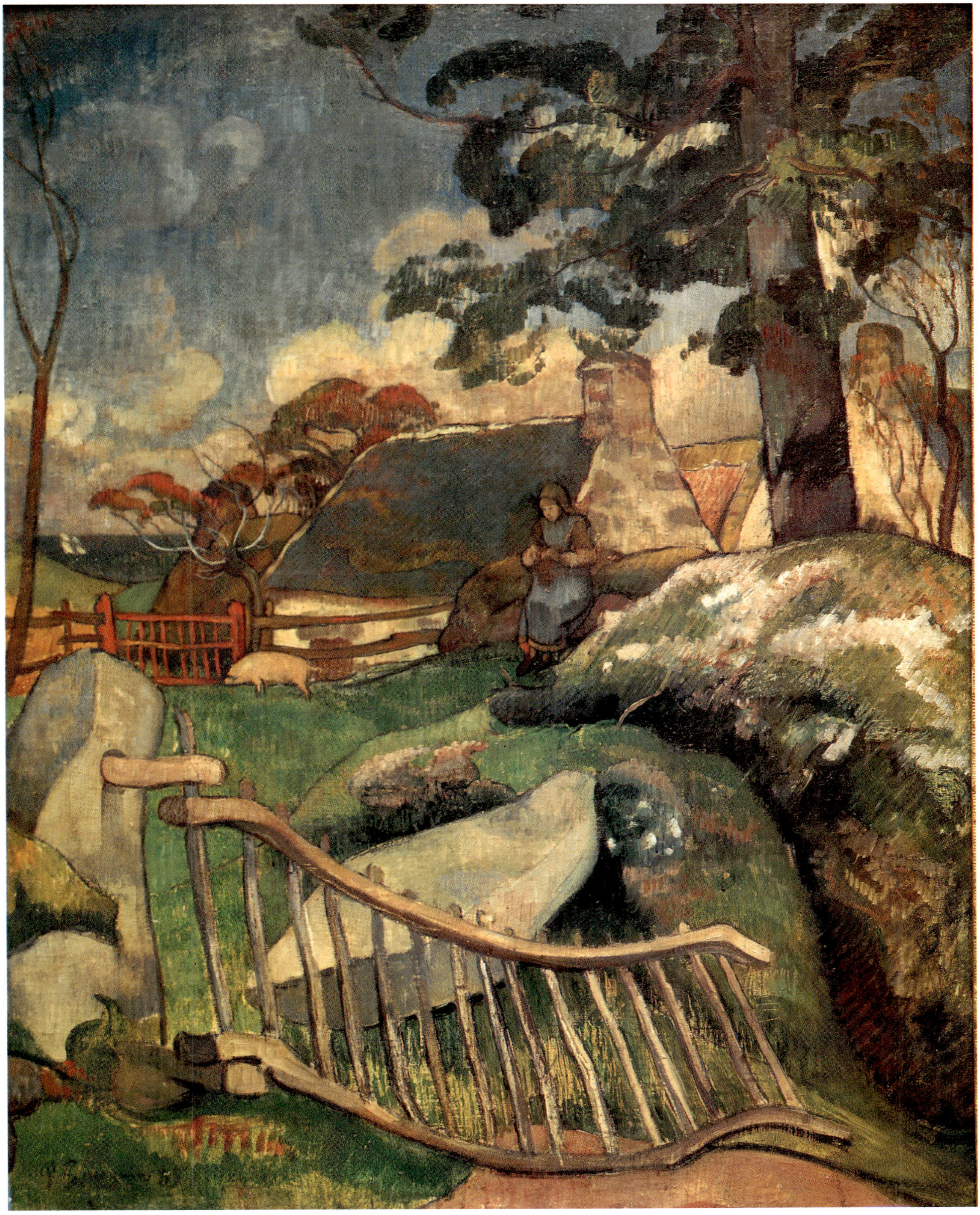

LA BARRIÈRE - THE FENCE
1889, Private collection
92 × 73 cm

mystical, in the certainty that "we have stripped everything of its mystery and luminosity: nothing is sacred any more." Jung dixit. Gauguin found his art of poetry in Brittany, accompanied and supported by young artists who already saw him as a door opening into another dimension of Impressionism. He was admired to self-destructive delirium by Van Gogh, spurred on by Mallarmé who believed him to be the great innovator. This was how he described the artist in the farewell dinner held in his honour at the Café Voltaire prior to his departure for the Marquesas. Years and years of learning and self-taught enquiry intervened between the youth shaken by his first contact with the Impressionists in Mr. Arosa's home, and this surly, deserted, virtually poverty-stricken man labouring under the burden of psychosomatic diseases, who was admired by small groups but despised in the art markets in which dealers and speculating collectors already reigned supreme. Rather than submerging ourselves in morbid accounts of Van Gogh's self-mutilation in chagrined response to Paul's desertion, we should, for the purposes of this enquiry, seek instead to follow as closely as we may the successive stages of the changes leading to the creation of Gauguin's poetics, nudging him along his southerly course, an established myth already in the Western culture created by the various literary manifestations of the imperial countries of the 19th century and transformed in the 20th century into a bauble of the spirit within reach of all nationalities. Mackintosh considers *Vision après le Sermon*, *Les Misérables*, *Manao Tupapau* and the inevitable

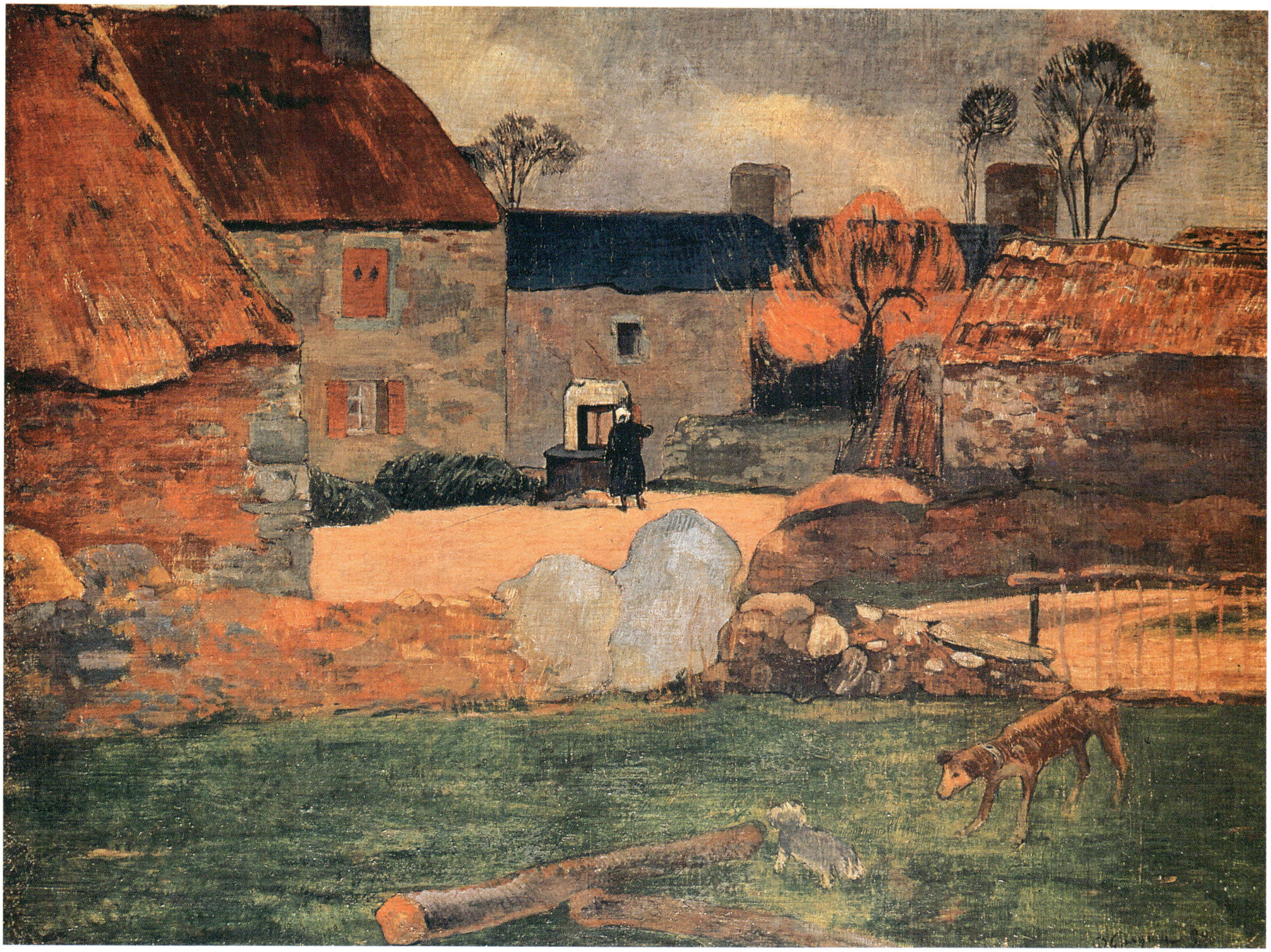

LE TOIT BLEU - THE BLUE ROOF
(or Pouldu Farm)
1890, Private collection
73 × 92 cm

Where do we come from? What are we? Where are we going? to constitute points of arrival on Paul Gauguin's artistic journey. Mackintosh maintains, however, that the artist's pictorial technique during his famous Polynesian period had been pre-established in Brittany and that the final journey was meaningful only in that it adhered to his particular brand of Symbolist activism: "In 1891, precisely when his stylistic innovations started to be more widely noted and imitated, he left France for the South Seas. He had come to understand that the crux of Symbolism ruled out the possibility of imbuing the picture with mystery and archetypal meaning if the traditions of French 19th-century painting are observed. Or, as the poet put it on another occasion: "You can't strike a match on a wall that has crumbled" and, despite the time he had spent in Brittany, he still felt hampered by the fetters of civilization."

It was not enough to possess nature, he needed natural landscapes that were uncorrupted by the utilitarian civilization which was destroying even Brittany. Tracing the course of Gauguin's artistic development from the time he stood awe-struck before Mr. Arosa's valiant collection, we must pause at *Les Maisons de Vaugirard* which is an outstanding work from his apprentice phase as an amateur painter (1880), or *Etude de Nu* (*Suzanne cousant*) of the same year and which was exhibited in 1881 in Paris and eight years later in Copenhagen, attracting the scorn of critics and of his wife's family alike. The Impressionist Gauguin improves consistently, until he begins to strike a

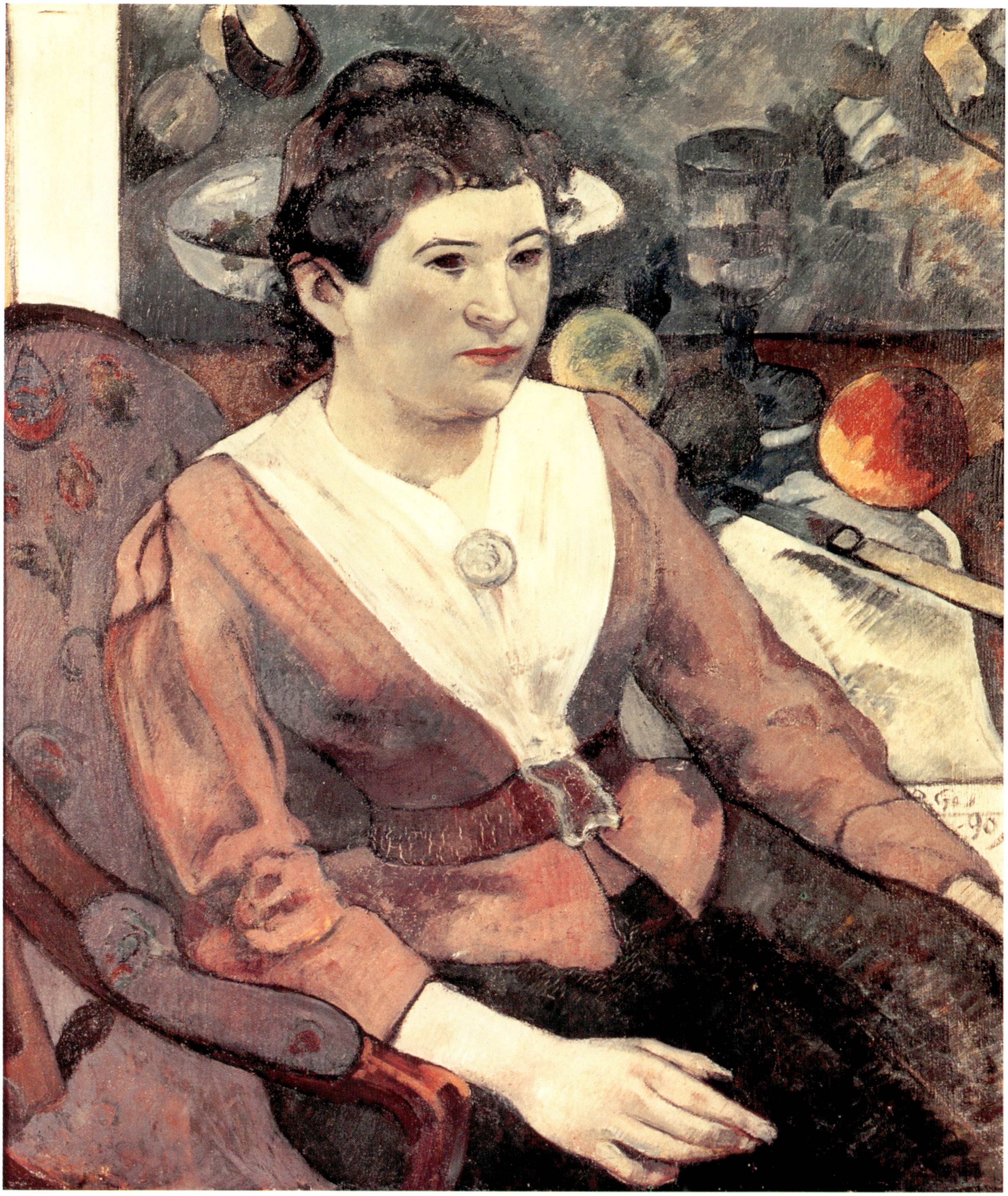

MARIE DERRIEN`A LA NATURE MORTE DE CÉZANNE - MARIE DERRIEN WITH CÉZANNE'S STILL LIFE
1890, Chicago, Art Institute
65 × 55cm

different note in works such as *Nature morte à la mandoline* (1885) or *La Plage du Pouldu* (1889) which are the beginning and end of his break with formalized Impressionism. In these paintings we see a rethinking of the fragmenting brush stroke, of the shape without outline and the attempt at direct reading in place of vaguely intimated meanings. In *La Plage du Pouldu* he opens the door to the colour of the Fauves and the abstract decorative composition of Art Nouveau. The Brittany period, which included the brief interludes in Panama and Martinique, places us squarely before a painter who has changed, producing allegorical paintings and native-inspired pottery upholding the virtues of popular crafts, contrary to Sèvres porcelain "which has killed the ceramic art." Today, the subject matter of the work that so irritated Pissarro, *Les Quatre Bretonnes,* would not be said to coincide with Maurice Barrès' reactionary exaltation of all that is Breton. It is more in the guise of an anthropologist's observation, sharing the opinion of Renan, another Breton, that Brittany is more deeply rooted in the past than the Lapp culture. This is not, however, meant by way of criticism but rather expresses the hope that this reserve of the pre-industrial indigenous population will remain untouched, but available to meet the demands of purity of Gauguin's eye and his meagre resources to cover food, accommodation and models at pre-industrial prices. *Les Meules ou Le Champ de pommes de terre* of 1890 is a structural approximation to Cézanne's figurative geometric style, which on occasion appears as a splendid decorative

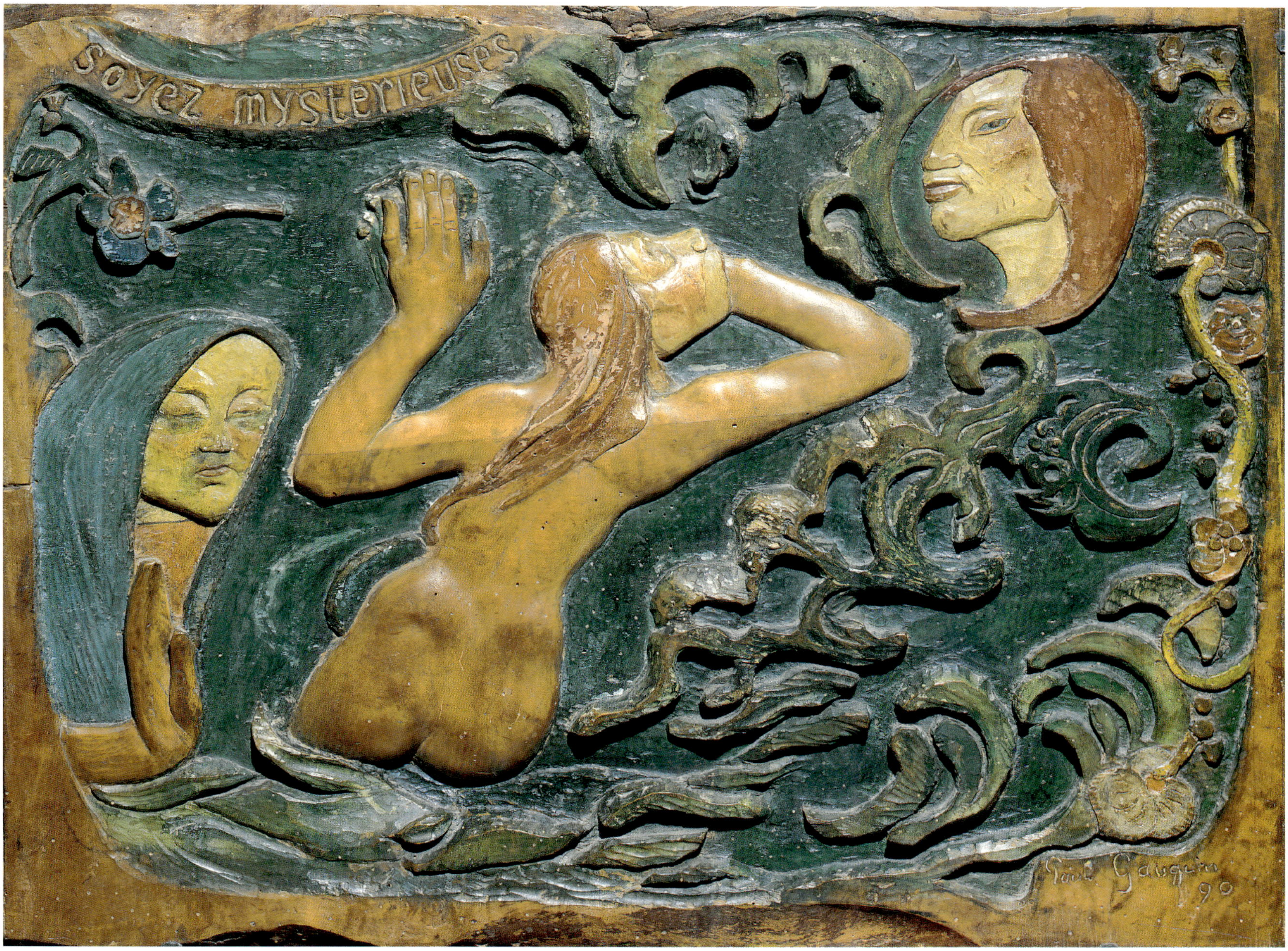

SOYEZ MYSTÉRIEUSES - BE MYSTERIOUS
1890, Paris, Musée d'Orsay
Multicoloured wood
73 × 95 × 0.5 cm

chromatic display, as beautiful as it is futile in *Végétation tropicale,* dated 1887 in Martinique, not far removed from the allegorical *Vision après le sermon* or *La Lutte de Jacob avec l'ange.* This was Gauguin's first religious painting and was turned down by a number of Breton churches. Even the progressive Impressionists put forward linguistic arguments to discredit the work. Whether in his Breton or in his Martinique phase, Gauguin adopts and discards the Impressionist technique according, as a rule, to the dictates of the subject or his impression of it. He would be an Impressionist for *Paysage breton avec cochon,* but cease to be so for *Jeunes Baigneurs bretons,* influenced by Degas' compositions and Puvis de Chavanne's nudes, to return to Symbolism in his scandalous *Sermon* and take his decorative landscape painting to Fauve extremes in *Marine avec vache au-dessus du gouffre.* Suddenly, during the course of that crazy year of 1888 during which he leapt from one style of painting to another, he created *Les Trois Petits Chiens,* one of his most polysemic works in which the effect of depth is destroyed and, virtually on the same plane, we see three little dogs around a casserole, three glasses, three apples and in the foreground a Cézanne-style vessel, making up a composition with virtually no perspective, in the Japanese-oriented style, serving a playful, secret argument. And in late October of that same year he painted *Les Alyscamps,* in Arles; an explosion of blazing colour in which he succeeds in balancing Van Gogh's chromatic outbursts, as he did also in *Ferme d'Arles or Les Arbres bleus.*

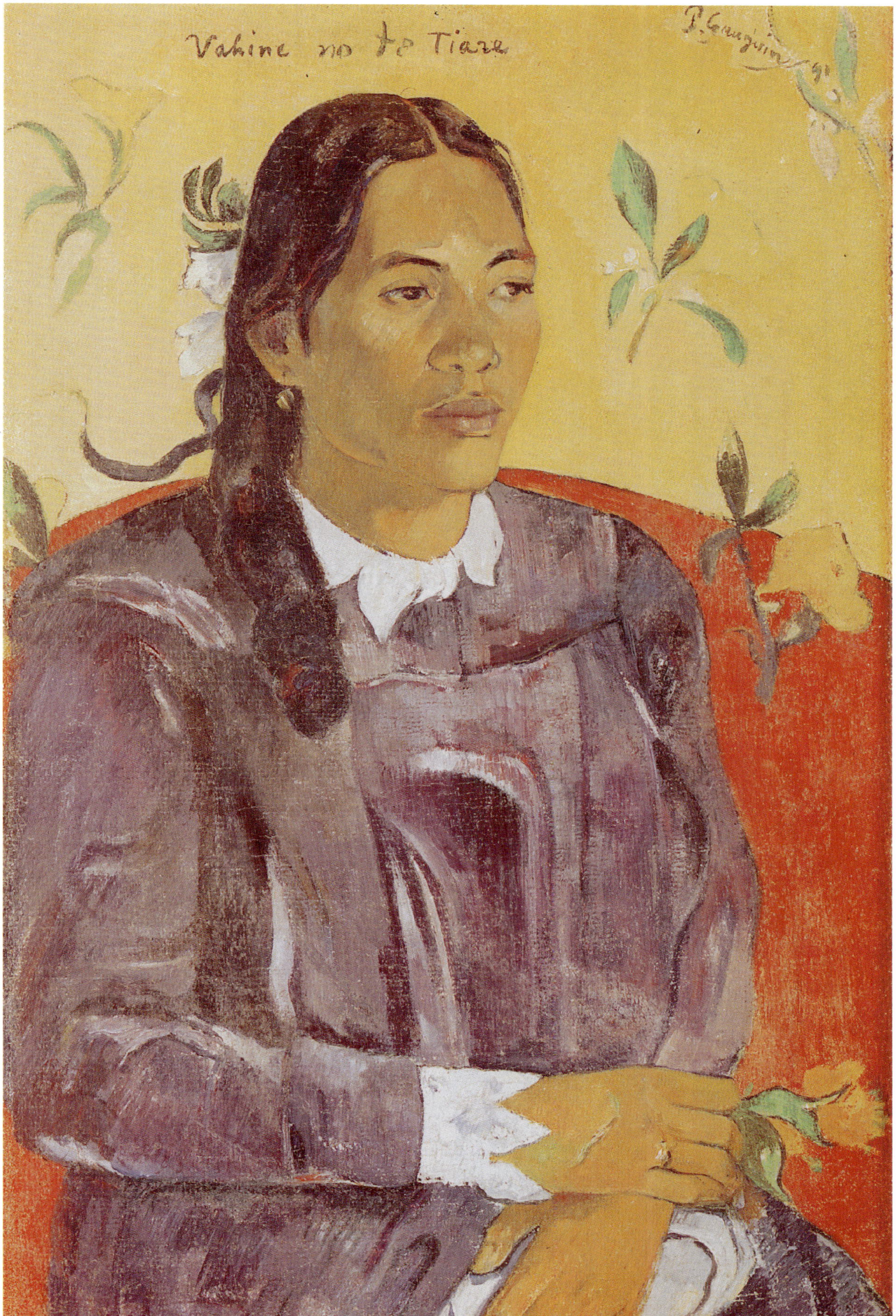

VAHINE NO TE TIARE
1891, Copenhaguen, Ny Carlsberg Glyptotek
70 × 46 cm

Back in Pont-Aven in 1889, Gauguin had become the definitive Gauguin, the painter whose name was associated in the popular mind with a handful of Polynesian paintings but who had already found his identity prior to travelling to the South Seas. Allegorical subjects, symbolic colour, compositions revealing a supreme decorative genius, regardless of the beauty or ugliness of the argument or of the components : *La Vie et la Mort, Dans les vagues, Petit Breton nu, Bonjour monsieur Gauguin* and the revolutionary *Christ jaune* over which Mallarmé and Mirbeau enthused, fully resolving to make Gauguin their plastic art representative, the visible head of post-Impressionist Symbolism. An alarming and delicious blend, wrote Mirbeau, of barbaric splendour, Catholic liturgy and Hindu enchantment, of Gothic imagery, of obscure and subtle symbolism... Looking at the picture today, one might consider it to be a particularly thorough and subtle colour test in every shade of yellow, with blue shadows, using the body of Christ as a vehicle. Why yellow? A colour test or perhaps a hyperbole of colour based on the ivory yellow of a Gothic Christ in multicoloured wood seen by Gauguin in a chapel near Pont-Aven. Although you could of course analyze it in strictly symbolic terms which state yellow to be a warm, forthcoming colour. According to psychoanalyst Dr. Jacobi, of the Jung school, yellow is the colour of the sun rising out of the shadows, like a messenger of light, and disappearing into the gloom "instantly lighting up the origins and course of events." In which case, colour symbolism is, I feel, somewhat haphazard and what

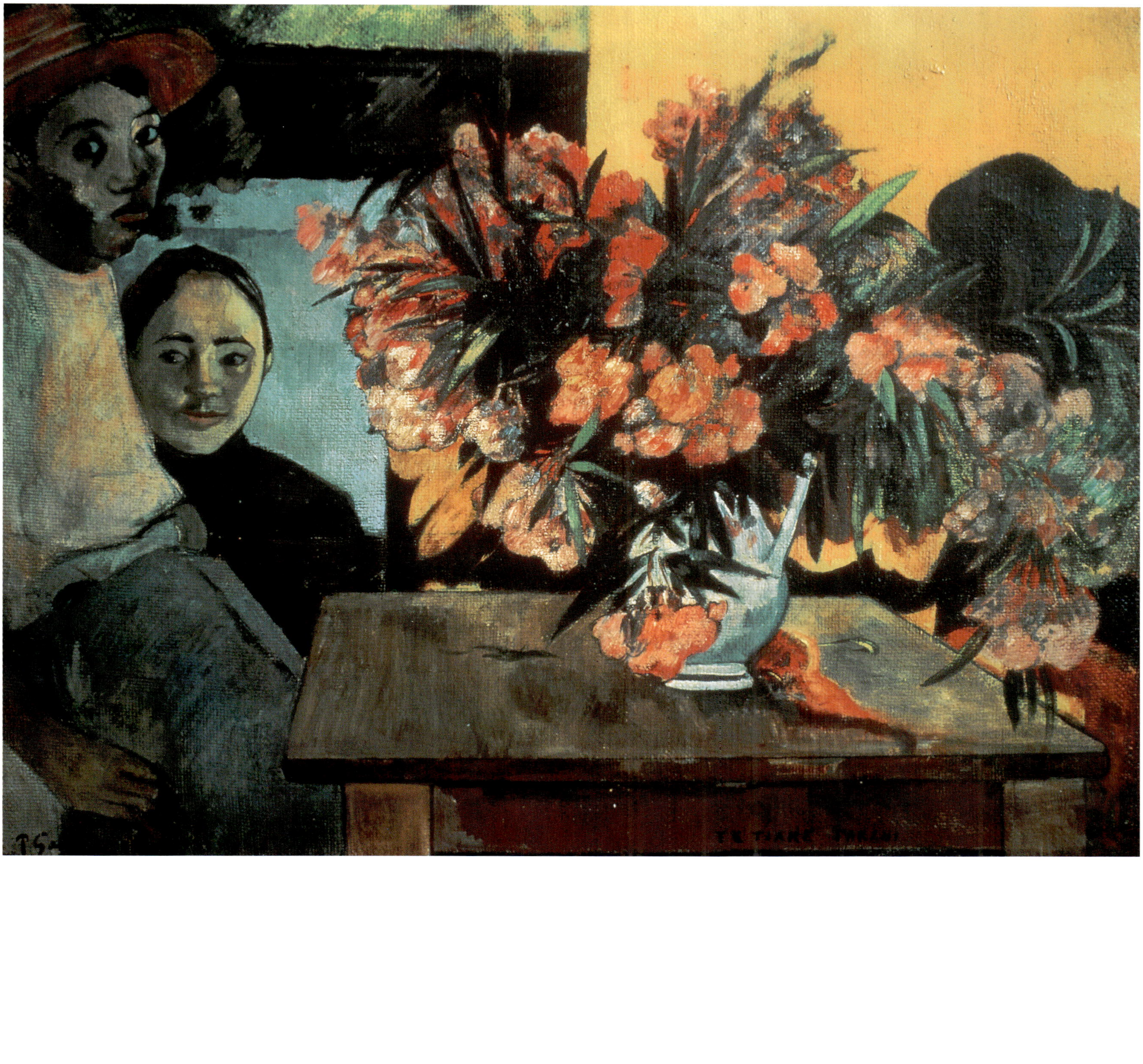

LE BOUQUET DE FLEURS - THE POSY OF FLOWERS
1891, Moscow, Pushkin Museum
95 × 62 cm

Gauguin was doing here was simply to create an experimental explosion of juxtaposed colours, in other words, a mere exercise in self-absorbed language.

From our vantage point a hundred years later, we see Gauguin possessed of a definitive language departing in March 1891 on his first journey to Polynesia, a journey which can only be explained as the logical conclusion of his life's motto, paraphrased from Latin: To live is not necessary, to travel is. Although Gauguin's pictorial imagination is one of argument and symbolism, it nonetheless requires real landscapes and models to work from. By 1891, Gauguin had exhausted all the possible combinations available in residual French primitivism. In his farewell speech, Mallarmé puts forward an acceptable motive for the trip and claims to admire "this proud awareness which, at the peak of his genius, sends him into exile, in quest of faraway places, in search of himself, to temper him anew." Mallarmé heaps praise on Gauguin, but to little avail because the prestige of the prince of French poets of the day does not bring in buyers, although it does win him the respect of the cultural establishment. Gauguin was aware that Mallarmé had elevated him to the ranks of the elite and was grateful. When he learned, in Tahiti, of the poet's death in 1898, he mourned him with more genuine sorrow than he showed on the death of his beloved Van Gogh in 1890. However, it is difficult to credit the hardened brutish Gauguin of that time with excessively cordial feelings towards friends he had manipulated to so little effect. The impetus of travel

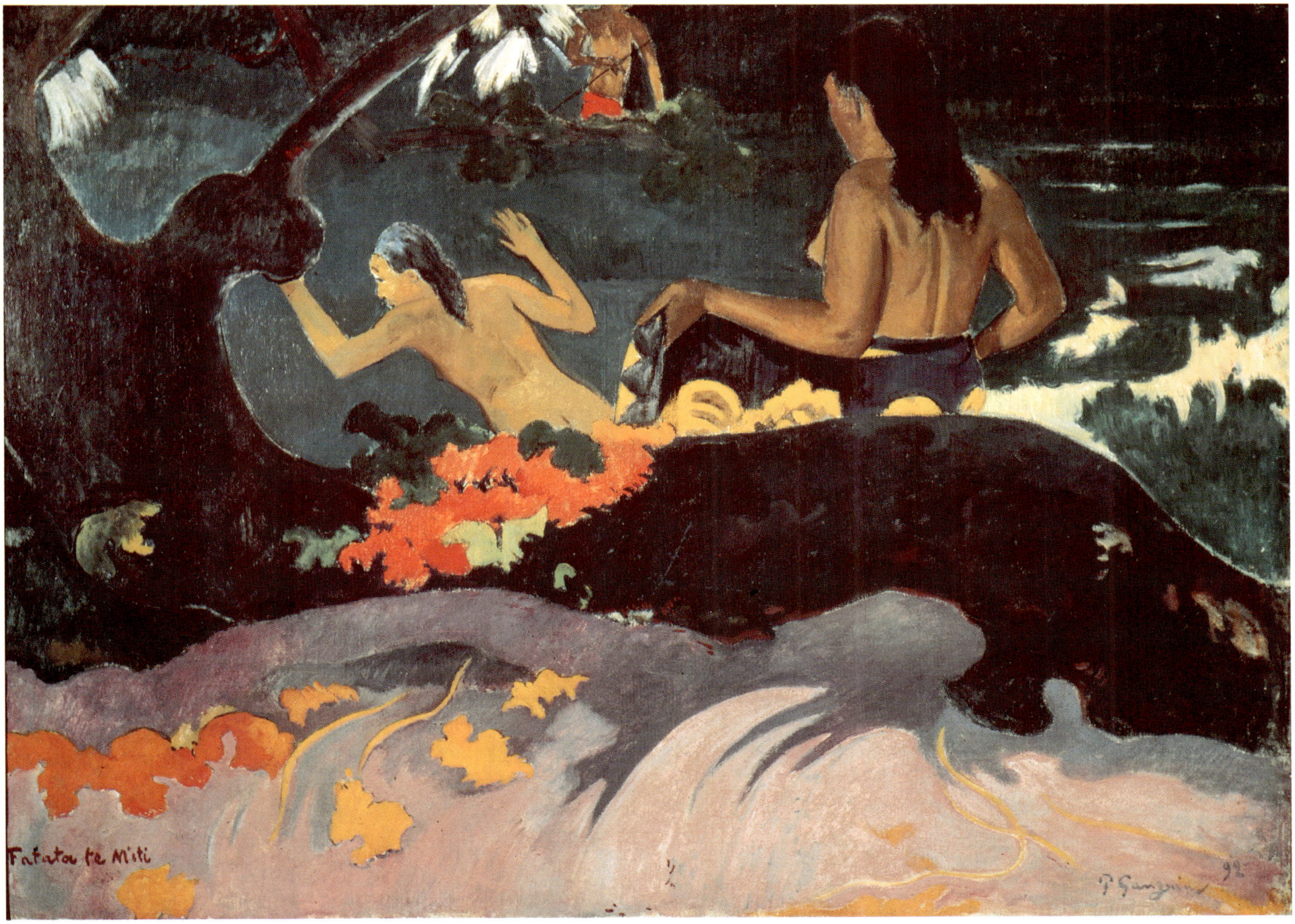

FATATA TE MITI
(Near the sea)
1892, Washington, National Art Gallery
68 × 92 cm

had eroded sentimental ties, he had broken off with Mette and while he kept up contact with his wife and children and fulfilled his financial obligations to them, he had become a proud recluse, suffering to be lauded by the elites, unshakably convinced of his own genius. He had mythicised his removal to the South Seas as the definitive encounter with the life forms and colours of the lost paradise of his childhood.

It was Van Gogh who had had the idea of creating a studio in the tropics, but in his conversations and letters Gauguin gradually appropriated the notion. After his Martinique experience, he was inclined to situate the tropics in Madagascar or in the Reunion Islands, until his friend Emile Bernard suggested Tahiti, reminding Paul of Van Gogh's attraction to the Marquesas as described in Pierre Loti's tales. Gauguin rediscovered his grandmother's utopian socialism and dreamed of creating an artists' phalanstery in the Marquesas. However, with Van Gogh's death, Gauguin's entourage in Brittany gradually lost heart. Bernard was the first to drop out. Although Gauguin felt too aged and weary to embark on such an endeavour alone, he persevered because his ideas were drying up. He concentrated his readings on the cultures and civilizations of the Antipodes and was gradually possessed of a belief that was to become prevalent during the 1960's: cultural eurocentrism has barred our access to other rationales of belief and behaviour, or social organisation and production. Gauguin turns his move away from wholesale utilitarian modernization into a progressive view of cultural

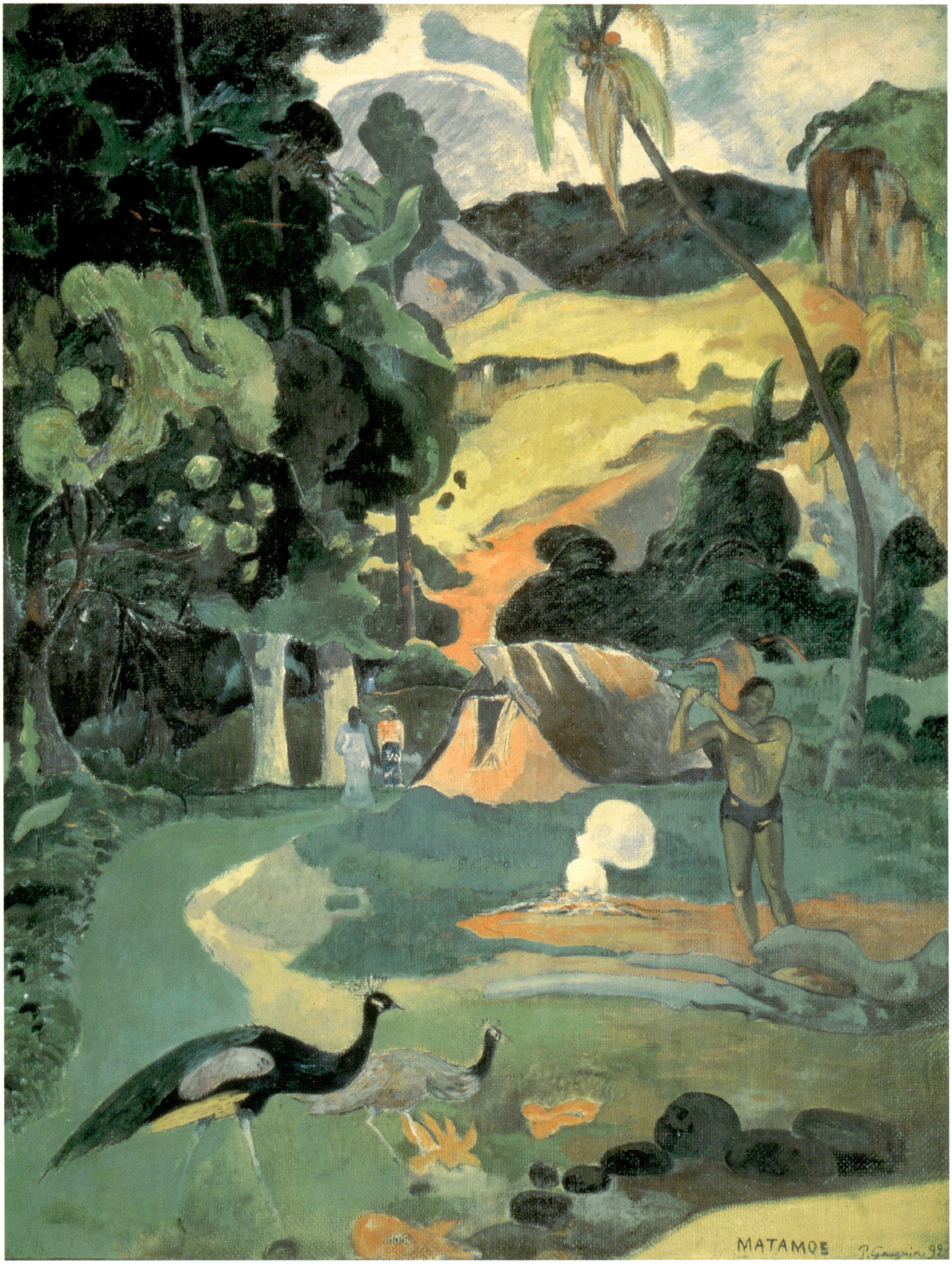

MATAMOE
(Landscape with peacocks)
1892, Moscow, Pushkin Museum
115 × 86 cm

polycentrism and an alternative to the capitalist model of society and mode of production. I must stress that he evades the dialectic collision with scientific or anarchic socialism and places himself outside the domain of the class struggle as instrument of change. Such is not his concern, however much he might despise a conformist society that humiliated him. Moreover, his flight to the Marquesas places him on a southerly course towards the cardinal point of warmth, bodily freedom and absence of cultural constraints on behaviour. Europeans were familiar with ethnological and literary works on Polynesia and the Anglo-Saxon culture of Melville and Eliot was in the process of creating the myth of the South as the impossible possibility of Paradise: "To read late into the night and to travel south in winter" is the vital aspiration of a character in one of Eliot's poems, surpassing the witness borne by such Anglo-Saxon intellectuals or artists who had fled South, no matter which South: Melville, Eliot, Hemingway, Malcolm Lowry, Paul Bowles, etc. Fugitives, imaginary or real, who assigned themselves to relative poverty soothed by the consistent rise of the dollar, even the fugitives' dollar. Gauguin did more than any of them, and did it in a more honest way, to open the eyes of the North towards the South, at a time when universal imperialism, or what we now call the international order, was being formalized. A time when the imperial powers, northern powers of course, gloated over their share of the booty of southern lands. Meanwhile, the international division of labour dictated that European workers would

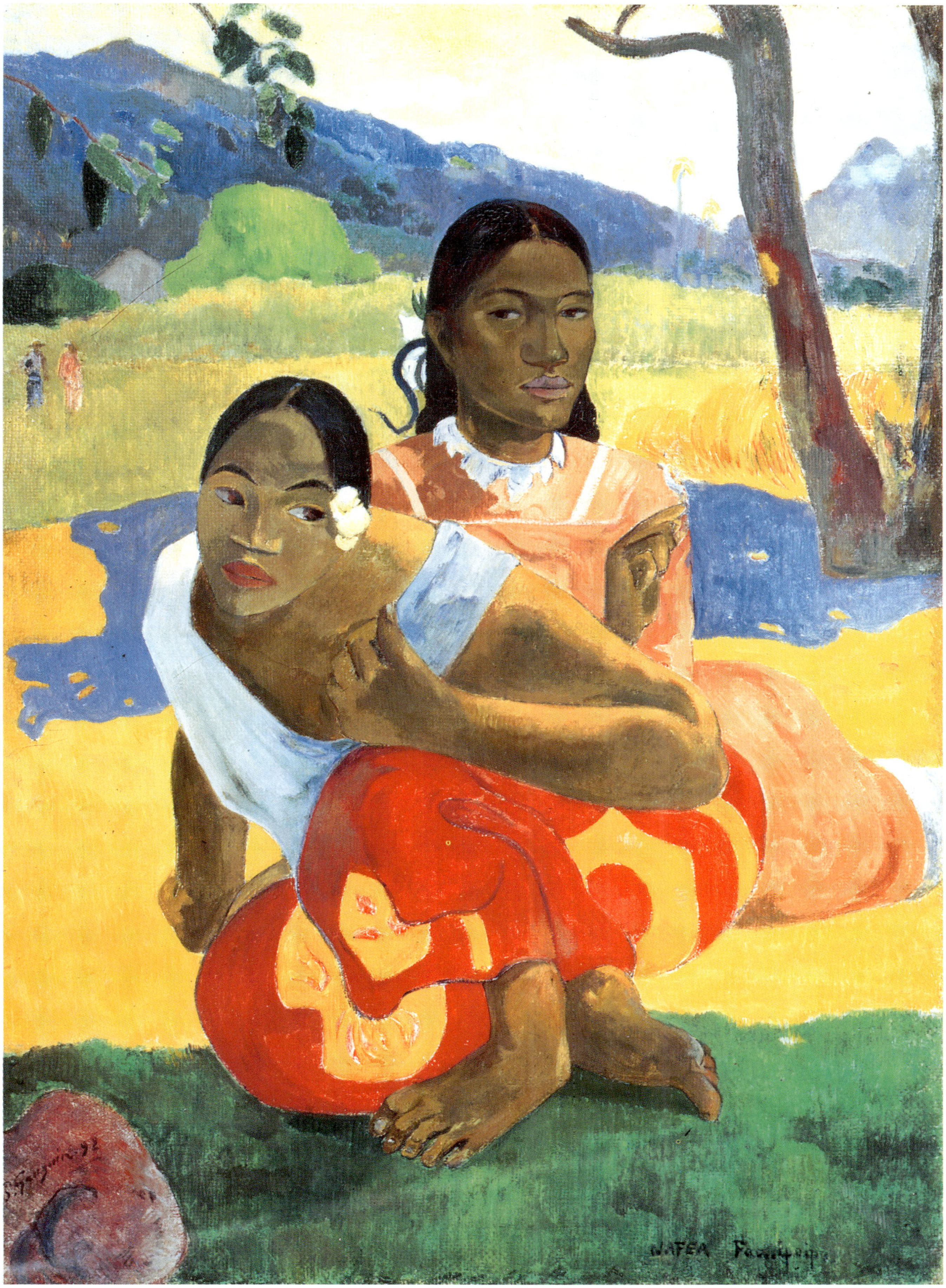

NAFEA FAA IPOIPO
(When do you marry?)
1892, Basel, Kunstmuseum, Öffentliche Kunstsammlung
101.5 × 77.5 cm

manufacture steel while the primitive Kanaka would pose for Gauguin, just as the Mexicans posed for Malcolm Lowry and the Spanish bull-fighters posed for Hemingway. "The West is rotten," said Gauguin, getting his word in before Spengler, and when he reached Tahiti he resolutely closed his eyes to indications that this paradise was already suffering the effects of colonialism, by the French in this instance.

Already, forty years previously, Herman Melville had been alarmed to see how the native propensity to live in paradise had been undermined by the cruelty and stupidity of the colonizers, with that typical American readiness to think that only others are imperialists. During the very period when the American whites were systematically exterminating the Indian nations, Melville was deeply concerned at the discrepancies he noted between what was recorded in the "log of the frigate Essex crossing the Pacific during the last war," and what his eyes beheld during that summer of 1842. "From then onwards our vessel was given over to excesses and debauchery of every type. No obstacles were placed in the way of the ungodly desires of the crew and their unbridled satisfaction. The most obscene licence and a shameful and general state of drunkenness were virtually unremitting during our vessel's stay in those ports. It is a disgrace indeed that these savages be exposed to such examples of corruption! They are so trusting and without hypocrisy that they readily succumb to vice of every type and their perdition, which mankind deplores, is inflicted on them by the Europeans

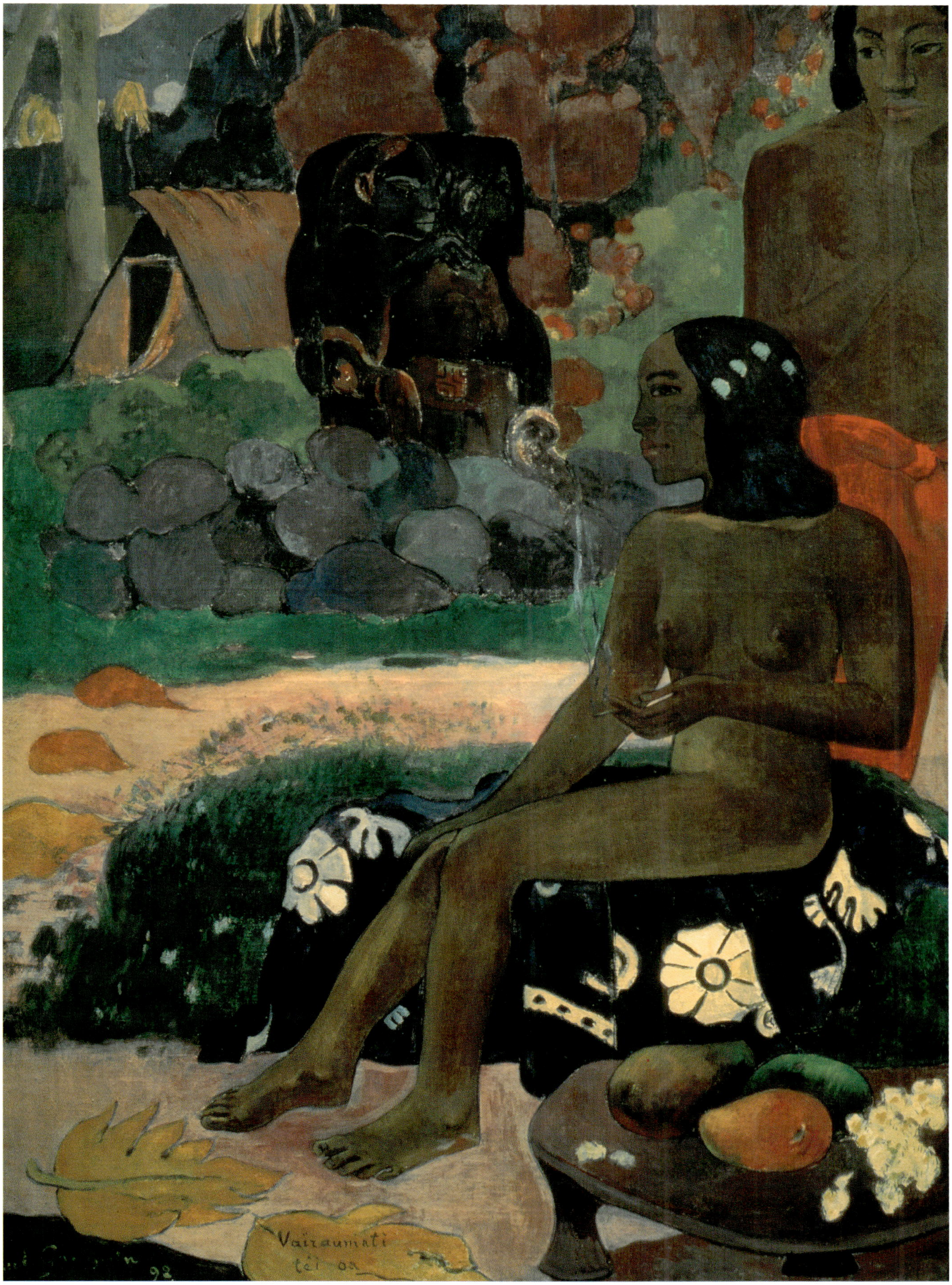

SON NOM EST VAIRAOUMATI · HIS NAME IS VAIRAOUMATI
1892, Moscow, Pushkin Museum
91 × 60 cm

supposedly bringing them the gist of civilization. Thrice blessed are those inhabiting some island lying undiscovered in the middle of the ocean who have not been subjected to the corrupting contact of the white man!" The indiscriminate extermination meted out by the colonizing races, for the mere pleasure of killing or intimidating, caused Melville to wonder whether the term savage was being correctly applied and he commented ironically that these "military" expeditions were subsequently held up in the West as proof of the providential superiority of a race or civilization. When he offered an enraptured description of Fayaway, the beautiful native girl, Melville put the finishing touches to the myth of the beauty of the Polynesian women which Gauguin was to carry with him on his final journey toward his own absolute, being the product, after all, of an education concentrating on the final and the absolute. "Luckless race!" exclaimed Melville. "I shudder to think how their paradisical existence will change in a few short years! And no doubt when the most destructive vices and the worst contributions of civilization have dispossessed the valley of the peace and happiness that previously reigned there, the magnanimous French will proclaim to the world that the Marquesas have been converted to Christianity!"

Gauguin reached the islands in time to see that Melville's fears were well-founded. Bengt Danielsson clearly showed how contradictory was the artist's sojourn in the South Seas, to which he was drawn by Mallarmé's cry, preceding that uttered by Eliot:

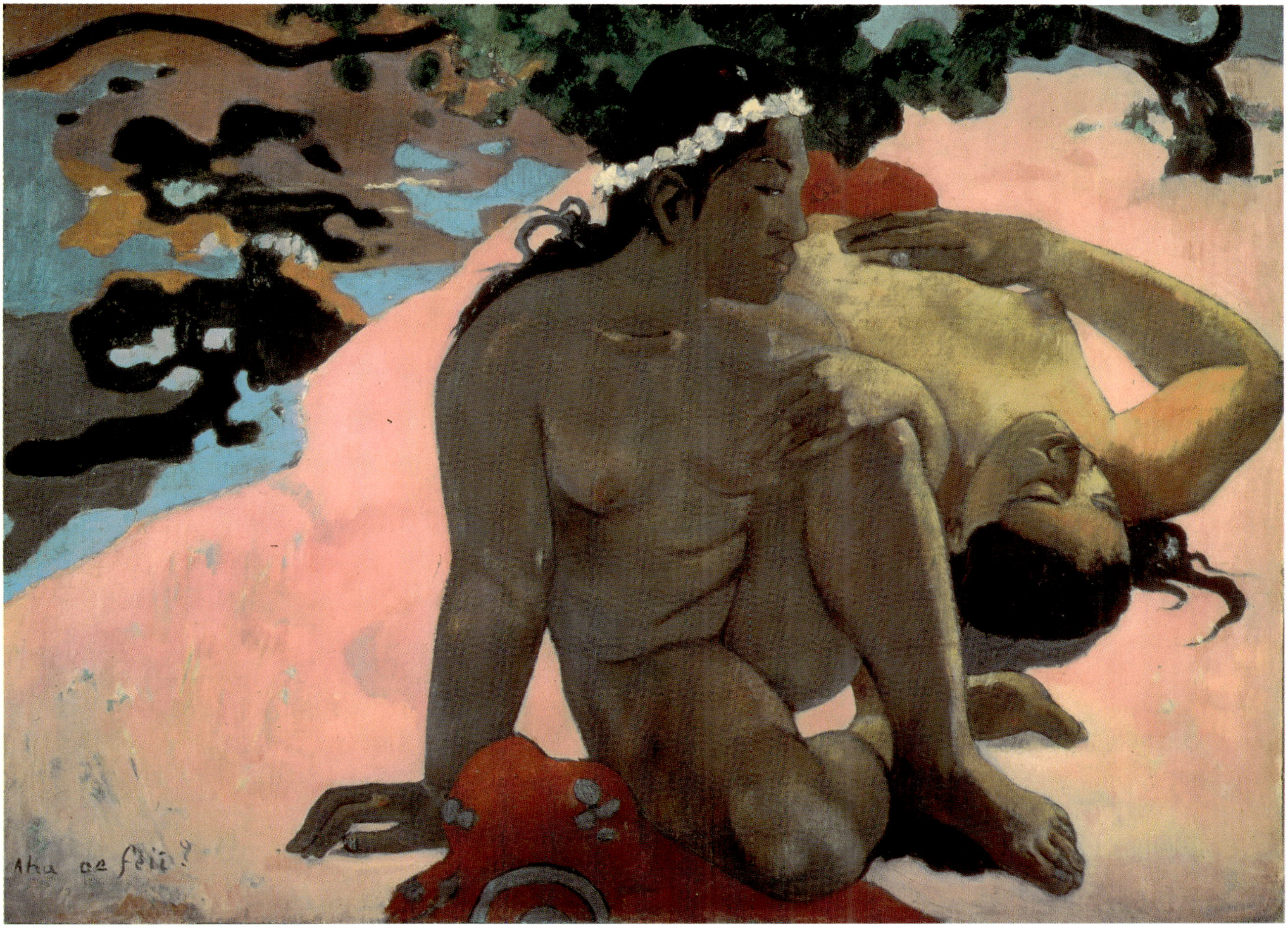

AHA OE FEII ?
(So what? Are you jealous?)
1892, Moscow, Pushkin Museum
68 × 92 cm

La chair est triste, hélas, et j'ai lu tous les livres
Fuir! Là-bas fuir! Je sens que des oiseaux sont ivres.

On June 9, 1891 Gauguin landed in Papeete, capital of Tahiti and of the Etablissements francais de l'Océanie. He had just turned forty-three and was realistic enough to see to what extent this hoped-for paradise had deteriorated. Papeete was a hybrid conglomeration of a town, a place of passage which had lost its native identity but failed to acquire a Western one to take its place. The houses were not of a kind you would expect to find in paradise, the people were not as beautiful as in ethnological illustrations, the only bare part of the women's bodies was their feet. When they set eyes on Gauguin with his long hair and artist's hat they took him for a *mahu*, or transvestite, of which there were a large number on the islands at that period. He was oppressed by Papeete and by the predatory and racist colonial population: "C'était l'Europe - L'Europe dont j'avais cru m'affranchir - sous les espèces aggravantes encore du snobisme colonial, d'une imitation puérile et grotesque jusqu'à la caricature. Ce n'était pas ce que je venais chercher de si loin." The painter made his way into the poor districts in pursuit of the golden bodies of the Kanaka... *l'or de leurs corps...* He drank and made love, only to weep before the photographs, hanging in his room, of Mette and his children, writing affectionate letters, symptomatic of his bad conscience, to his startled wife. He made his way inland seeking a more primitive lifestyle, an authenticity no longer to be found in the capital. But

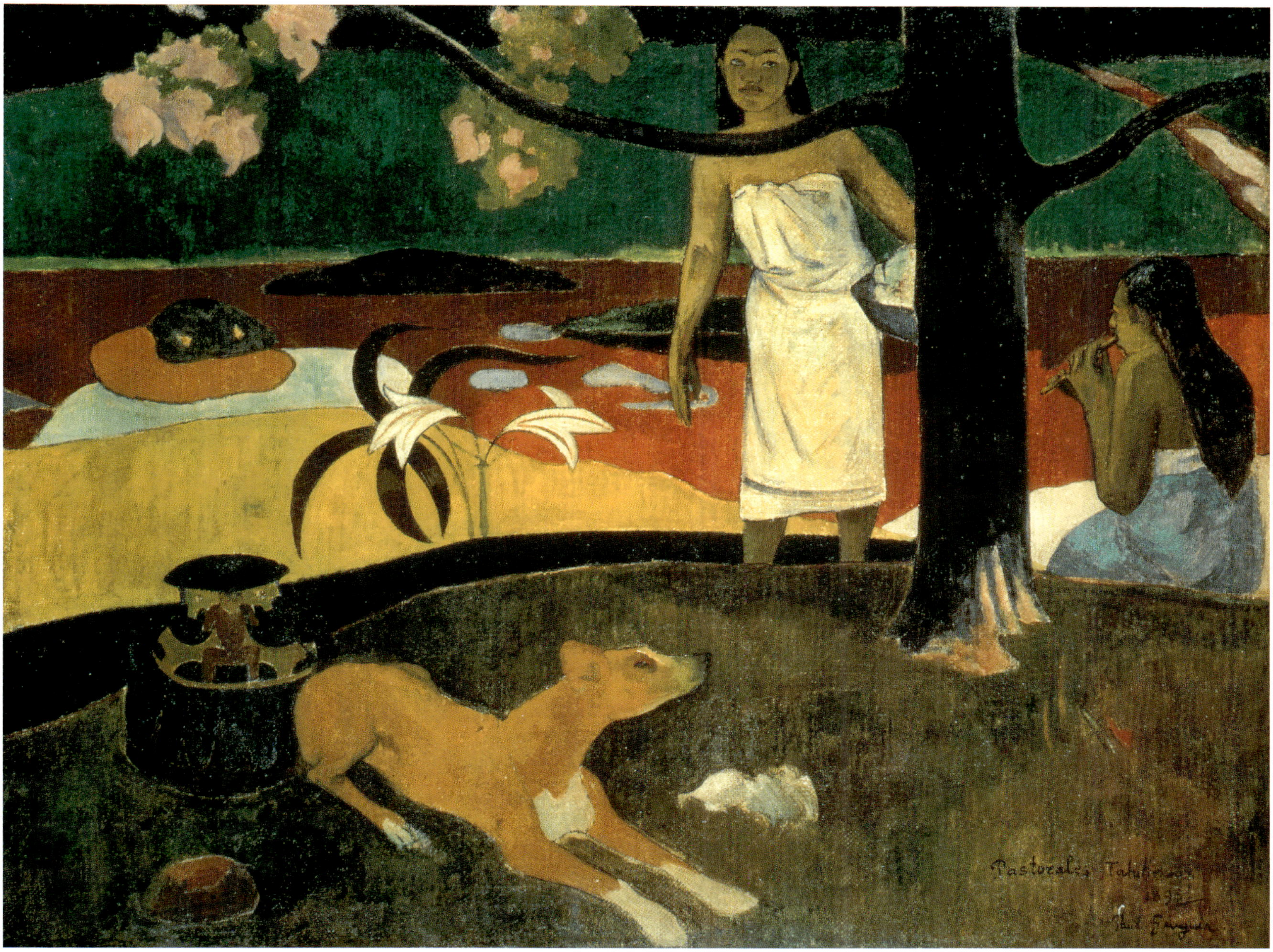

PASTORALES TAHITIENNES - PASTORAL TAHITIAN SCENES
1893, Leningrad, Hermitage Museum
87.5 × 113.7 cm

the white man had forestalled him here also, whether in the guise of missionary, landowner or soldier and nobody understood the innocence with which this painter, who was so little inclined to follow the academic road, sought to repossess the original innocence of people and objects. In the countryside, in the jungle, in the coastal villages, Gauguin occasionally encountered people and situations similar to those of which he had dreamed and, though they might not coincide exactly, his creative imagination made good the difference. He painted, he scraped a living, he sold paintings neither on the island nor back in the metropolis from which the mail ships returned without the cheques he was expecting. He was obliged to work as a guard in a furniture warehouse, but his illusions held strong while his dreams crumbled and several dozen paintings bear virtuous witness to the rightness of his coming to the island. These paintings contribute nothing new in the technical sense, but Tahiti offered him a feast of primitive raw material to glut the deprivation he had felt in France prior to his trip. The fact that he was creatively engaged permitted him to bear with his poverty, his illnesses, the official reprimand he had received for bathing naked in Mataeia. He had offended the modesty of the colony, not that of the natives. He corresponded with his friends and family, sent samples of his work and in Paris he was seen as an art correspondent of the South Seas. Although the Polynesian period was not one of technical or linguistic progress in his manner of expression, it did nonetheless afford him the op-

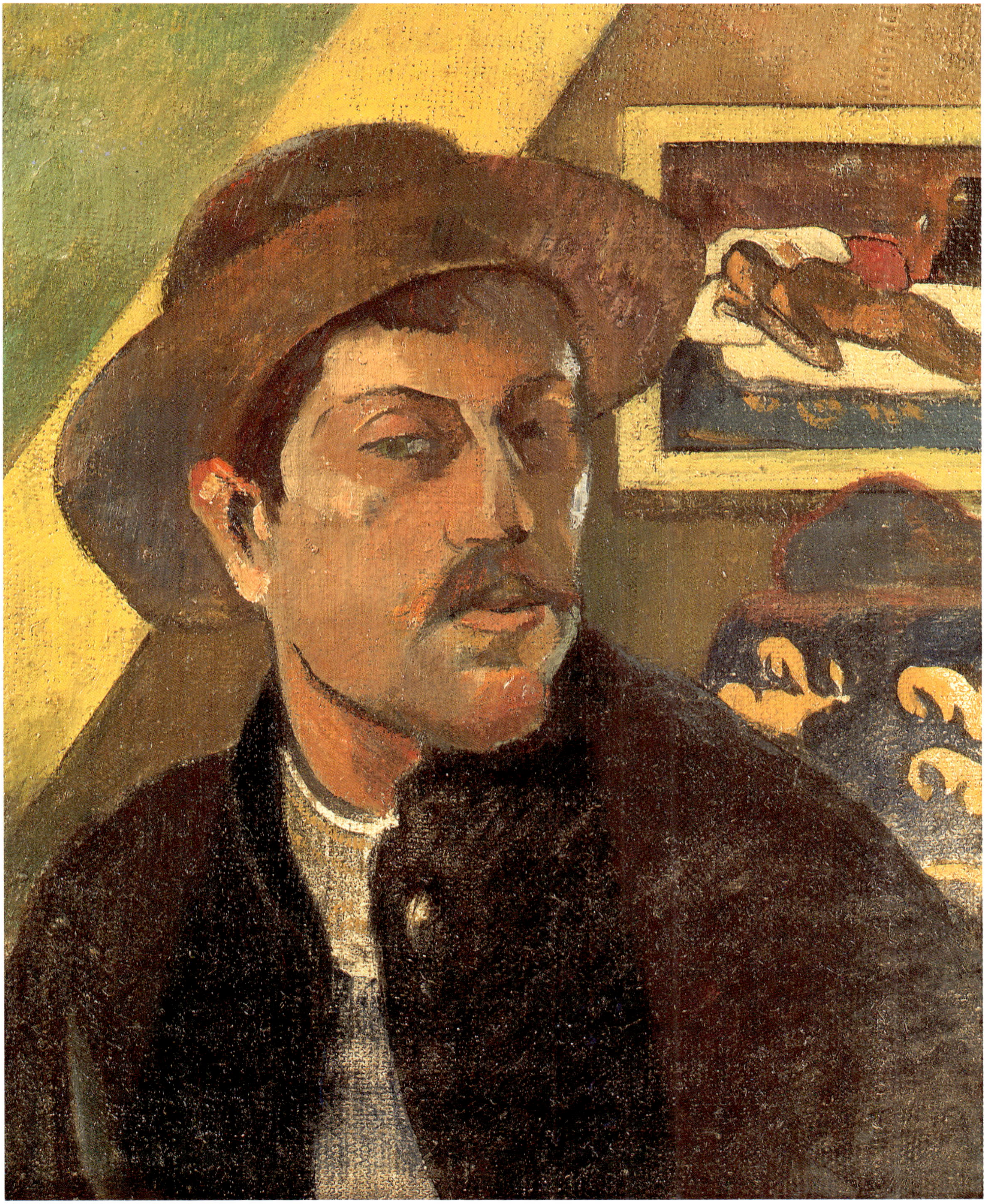

AUTOPORTRAIT AU CHAPEAU - SELF-PORTRAIT WITH HAT
1893-1894, Paris, Musée d'Orsay
46 × 38 cm